CHAPTER

IN A

VERSE

BY PHILLIP WITHERIDGE

Contents

Preface

What's the deal with this book?

Over the past year, I've been reading roughly three chapters of the bible every day. After reading each chapter, I'd write a very short summary of what the chapter's about. When I finished, I thought it'd be a good idea to put all the summaries together, and read them from start to finish. After reading through the summaries, from Genesis to Revelation, I felt like I understood the basic flow and plot of the bible better. And that's the point of this book. I think this book will help people understand the flow and plot of the bible better.

The book is easier read in some sections than others. This will become evident as you read through. Overall, I think the book is most helpful in outlining the narrative sections of the bible. The Old Testament historical books section is easier to read, in my opinion, than the non-linear wisdom and prophetic books section. It doesn't mean you shouldn't read the non-linear wisdom and prophetic section summaries, but it might take more time to let it all sink in.

Generally, if you see *He*, *His*, or *Him* with a capital 'H', not as the starting word of a sentence, I'm talking about God and/or Jesus.

When it comes to the New Testament epistles, I decided to use "we" and "Christians" interchangeably.

The layout is simple. The verse numbers that you see at the start of some sentences are actually chapter numbers. For example:

*[1]**God creates** the universe in six days and rests on the seventh. [2]He creates **Adam and Eve** and places them in the Garden of Eden. [3]Adam and Eve are deceived by a serpent, and they **sin** against God by eating forbidden fruit. God pronounces curses on them and puts them out of the garden.*

In this example, we see the first three chapters of Genesis summarised. The verse numbers correspond to the chapter being summarised. I decided to bold certain words and phrases to emphasise what I believe to be key points in the plot of a particular book. This can be seen in the example above. You'll see this more clearly in the full text.

I need to make a three points clear about this book:

1) It is not perfect. It is an imperfect tool which has helped me understand the flow and plot of the bible, and I hope it will help others in the same way. It is not comprehensive. It is not complete. But it is helpful.

2) It is not a substitute for the bible. The best way to understand the flow and plot of the bible is to read the bible in its entirety. This book is a reference tool and a basic plot guide. It shouldn't be used as a substitute for regular bible reading and study.

3) It might take a while to get, but it's worth it. This book may be hard to read in many sections. Chapters might seem to get repetitive. On the other hand, chapters might seem to have no connection to the ones preceding. But it's worth reading this book slowly and carefully, because the bible is like that. At times, the bible seems to get repetitive. At times, it seems to bounce off events and themes which don't seem to have any natural connection. And this is reflected in this book. Through study and perseverance, I think readers will be lead, like I have been, to a better understanding of the flow and plot of the bible.

I have been helped greatly by this book to further my understanding of the bible – it's structure, content, and flow. I hope it is helpful to others as well.

OLD TESTAMENT

HISTORY

Genesis

[1]**God creates** the universe in six days and rests on the seventh. [2]He creates **Adam and Eve** and places them in the Garden of Eden. [3]Adam and Eve are deceived by a serpent, and they **sin** against God by eating forbidden fruit. God pronounces curses on them and puts them out of the garden.

[4]Eve gives birth to **Cain and Abel**, and Cain kills Abel. [5]Adam's son Seth bears descendants that lead down to Noah.

[6]God decides to blot out mankind, except for **Noah**, and He commands Noah to build an ark. [7]Noah builds the ark and enters it with his family and many animals, and a **flood** covers the Earth. [8]The flood subsides and Noah exits the ark with his family and the animals. [9]God establishes a **covenant** with Noah. Sadly, Noah shamefully gets drunk soon after. Noah's grandson Canaan is cursed, and Noah dies. [10]Noah's descendants are outlined.

[11]The people of the Earth build the **Tower of Babel** in an act of pride, so God confuses their languages and disperses them over the whole Earth.

[12]God tells **Abram** (a tenth-generation descendant of Noah) to leave his home to go to a land that God will show him. Abram complies and goes to Canaan with his wife Sarai and his nephew Lot. God promises to give the land of Canaan to Abram's offspring, and the group sojourns to

Egypt. [13]They leave Egypt and Abram separates from his nephew Lot. Abram settles in Canaan while Lot settles in Sodom.

[14]Foreign kings attack Lot's hometown Sodom, but Abram and his men save them, so Melchizedek the High Priest blesses Abram. [15]God establishes His **covenant** with Abram, assuring him that his many offspring will inherit the land of Canaan. [16]Abram's barren wife Sarai tells Abram to have a child with their servant Hagar, so Abram does, and Hagar gives birth to Ishmael.

[17]God changes Abram's name to **Abraham**, and establishes the **covenant of circumcision** with him. God changes Sarai's name to Sarah, and promises her a child of her own, who will be called Isaac. [18]God appears to Abraham and assures him that Sarah will have a son. He also says He will survey Sodom and Gomorrah and will destroy them if there are no righteous people there.

[19]God brings Lot out of Sodom with his wife and daughters, and then destroys **Sodom and Gomorrah**. Lot's wife looks back and turns into a pillar of Salt. Lot's two daughters sleep with Lot, and become pregnant.

[20]Abraham sojourns in Gerar and tells people that Sarah is his sister, to protect her. The king of Gerar takes Sarah, but is told by God that Sarah is in fact Abraham's wife, so he returns her to Abraham and reconciles with Abraham. [21]Sarah gives birth to **Isaac**. God promises Hagar that her son Ishmael will become a great nation. Abraham establishes a covenant of peace with the king of Gerar, and then sojourns in the land of the Philistines.

[22]God tells Abraham to **sacrifice** his son Isaac. As Abraham is about to sacrifice Isaac, God provides an animal sacrifice for Abraham, who proved his faithfulness to God. [23]Sarah dies and is buried by Abraham. [24]Abraham tells a servant to go and get a wife for Isaac, so the servant goes outside Canaan and gets Rebekah, who comes back to Isaac and becomes his wife. [25]Abraham dies and is buried. Isaac's wife Rebekah gives birth to **Jacob and Esau**, and Esau sells his birthright to Jacob. [26]Isaac sojourns in Gerar and establishes a covenant of peace with Abimelech king of Gerar. [27]Jacob pretends to be Esau so that his father Isaac would bless him. The plan works, and Esau is furious with Jacob.

[28]Isaac sends Jacob to Laban (Rebekah's brother) to find a wife. [29]Jacob works for Laban, but is tricked into sleeping with Leah (Laban's older daughter), but he continues to work and eventually marries his true love Rachel (Laban's younger daughter). [30]Leah and one of her servants, and Rachel and one of her servants, bear Jacob the following sons: **Reuben, Simeon, Levi, Judah, Dan, Naphtali, Gad, Asher, Issachar, Zebulon, and Joseph** (these make up eleven of the twelve tribes of Israel). [31]Jacob realises that Laban no longer sees him with favour, so he flees with his wives towards Canaan. Laban pursues him, catches up to him, and they establish a covenant of peace with one another. [32]Jacob wrestles with God on his way to Canaan, and his name is changed to **Israel**.

[33]Israel and Esau joyfully reunite, and Israel arrives at Canaan safely. [34]The Hivites (neighbours of the Israelites in Canaan) are tricked and defeated in battle by the sons of Jacob, following the rape of Dinah (a daughter of Israel) by Shechem (a Hivite). [35]Rachel dies while giving birth to **Benjamin**, who is to become the twelfth tribe of Israel. Isaac also dies. [36]Esau's descendants are outlined.

[37]**Joseph** is hated by his brothers, and is sold to traders. They take him to **Egypt** to be a servant of Potiphar, an officer of Pharaoh. [38]Judah impregnates his own daughter-in-law, who he thought was a roadside prostitute. [39]Potiphar's wife tries to seduce Joseph, but he resists the temptation. Potiphar's wife then accuses Joseph of abuse, so he is put into prison. [40]Joseph interprets a few dreams of Pharaoh's servants, but when they retire they forget about him. [41]Joseph interprets one of Pharaoh's dreams, revealing that there will be seven years of prosperity followed by seven years of famine in Egypt. Pharaoh appoints Joseph to be second in command over Egypt. **Manasseh and Ephraim** are born to Joseph.

[42]The **famine** begins, and people start to come to Egypt to buy supplies. Ten of **Joseph's brothers** come and try to buy supplies, but Joseph recognises them and tells them that unless they also bring the eleventh brother (Benjamin) with them, he won't let them buy. They go back home and tell this to Israel, who is extremely anxious about the whole thing. [43]Joseph's brothers bring Benjamin to Egypt. [44]Joseph tests his brothers' integrity by putting a valuable item in their bags that doesn't belong to them, and they come back to Egypt and tell the truth to Joseph. [45]Joseph reveals himself as Joseph to his brothers, and they all rejoice. Joseph's brothers go up to Canaan to bring their father Israel down to Egypt to live there with Joseph.

[46]Joseph's father and brothers come to Egypt, and [47]Joseph gives his family land to settle in. [48]Israel blesses Ephraim and Manasseh (Joseph's sons), and [49]blesses his sons who will make up the twelve tribes of Israel. **Israel dies** and is buried. [50]After burying Jacob, Joseph reassures his

brothers that they are forgiven for what they have done in that past to Joseph, and that God has used all that has happened for good. **Joseph dies** and is buried.

Exodus

[1]A new **Pharaoh** rises up in Egypt and oppresses the Israelites. [2]**Moses** is born and is hidden from Pharaoh. He grows up and hides in Midian. [3]God appears to Moses in the form of a **burning bush**, and tells Moses to command Pharaoh to **let the Israelites go**. [4]Moses doubts God's ability to speak through him, so God gives Moses a helper called Aaron. Moses and Aaron go to Egypt.

[5]Moses and Aaron tell Pharaoh to let the Israelites go, but **Pharaoh refuses**. [6]God reassures Moses that He will bring the Israelites out of Egypt. [7]God sends **plagues** upon Egypt. He makes the Nile turn into blood, but Pharaoh's heart remains hardened. [8]Frogs, gnats and flies cover Egypt, but Pharaoh hardens his heart. [9]The livestock of the Egyptians die, boils and hail oppress Egypt, [10]locusts and darkness cover Egypt, but God hardens Pharaoh's heart. [11]God threatens the death of every Egyptian firstborn, but He hardens Pharaoh's heart. [12]The **Passover** is established for Israel, God strikes down all Egyptian firstborns, and Pharaoh tells Moses and Aaron to take Israel and leave Egypt.

[13]Moses exhorts Israel to always remember that it is God who brought them out of Egypt. [14]The Israelites cross the **Red Sea** while the Egyptians are crushed by it. [15]Israel sings a song of praise to God, and God turns bitter water into sweet water for the Israelites. [16]The Israelites grumble about not having any food, and God rains bread from heaven for them. [17]Strong people called the Amalek come and fight against Israel, but Joshua (Moses' assistant) gets an army together and defeats the Amalek.

[18]Jethro (Moses' father-in-law) tells Moses to delegate judicial responsibilities to other faithful men, because the job is too hard for Moses to do alone. [19]The Israelites arrive at **Mount Sinai** and Moses goes up the mountain to be spoken to by God.

[20]God gives Moses the **Ten Commandments**. [21-22]God gives laws about civil matters and [23]promises that Israel will enter Canaan. [24]Moses tells Israel God's laws, and they promise to obey. [25]God tells Moses that Israel is to build a **sanctuary for God**, that He may dwell in their midst. He tells them to build the Ark of the Covenant, the table for bread, a golden lamp stand, [26]the tabernacle, [27]the bronze altar and the tabernacle court. [28]God tells them that Aaron and his sons are to be priests in the land of God's people, and He outlines what they are to wear. [29]God explains how the priests are to be consecrated and ordained. [30]God tells them to build the altar of incense and the bronze basin, and he explains the census rules to them. [31]God appoints able men to build everything, and He reminds Israel of the Sabbaths.

[32]Israel makes a **golden calf** as an idol, and God gets angry at them. **Moses pleads** with God not to destroy Israel, and **God relents** and decides not to destroy Israel. [33]God again says that Israel will leave Sinai and enter **Canaan**, and Moses builds the tent of meeting. [34]God renews his **covenant** with Israel, and [35]all the people of Israel bring contributions for the construction of the sanctuary. [36]Israel builds the tabernacle, [37]the Ark of the Covenant, the table for bread, the golden lamp stand, the incense altar, [38]the burnt offering altar, the bronze basin, and the court. [39]They make the priests' garments and [40]erect the tabernacle. All the work is finished, and God's glory fills the temple.

Leviticus

[1]**God speaks to Moses** from the tent of meeting. He tells him about burnt offerings, [2]grain offerings, [3]peace offerings, [4]sin offerings, and [5]guilt offerings. [6]He tells him about the priests' responsibilities related to the offerings, and [7]He tells him to tell all of Israel about the offerings. [8]Moses consecrates Aaron and his sons as Priests, and [9]Aaron blesses Israel. [10]Sadly, two of Aaron's sons present unauthorized sacrifices to God, and God kills them.

[11]God tells Moses about what they can eat. [12]He tells him about how to become clean after childbirth.

[13-14]He tells him about the rules for people with leprosy and skin diseases, and [15]about becoming clean after bodily discharges. [16]He tells him about the Day of Atonement: an annual event involving sacrifice where all sins are atoned for.

[17]God tells Moses about: the rules about eating blood, [18]unlawful sexual relations, [19]loving your neighbour as yourself, [20]the punishments for child sacrifice and sexual immorality, and [21]the need for priests to be holy.

[22]God tells Moses the difference between acceptable and unacceptable offerings. [23]He tells him about the Sabbath day, the Passover, the Feast of Firstfruits, the Feast of Weeks, the Feast of Trumpets, the Day of Atonement, and the Feast of Booths. [24]He tells him about the punishment for blasphemy, and the "eye for an eye" principle. [25]He tells

him about the Sabbath year (the seventh year) and the year of Jubilee (the fiftieth year). [26]He tells him about the blessings for covenantal obedience and the punishments for disobedience, and [27]He tells him about the laws about vow-making.

Numbers

[1]God tells Moses to take a census of the people of Israel. [2]He tells him how to arrange the camps of Israel by clan. [3]The sons of Aaron and the ministerial duties of the Levites are outlined. [4]God tells Moses to take a census of the sons of Kohath, the sons of Gershon, and the sons of Merari (all sons of Levi). God outlines these groups' roles within Israel. [5]God tells Moses about individual confession and restitution, and talks about the procedures for suspected adultery. [6]He tells him about the Nazirite Vow, which involves separation to God in holiness in a unique way. [7]The chiefs of Israel bring offerings before the tabernacle, [8]God tells Moses to cleanse the Levites, [9]Israel celebrates the Passover, [10]Moses makes trumpets useful for summoning all of Israel, and **Israel leaves Sinai and heads for Canaan**.

[11]Israel complains about a lack of food. God tells Moses to delegate some of his burdens to seventy faithful men. [12]Miriam and Aaron confront Moses because he married a Cushite woman, but God defends Moses. [13]God tells Moses to send men to spy out the land of Canaan. The spies go, and they bring back a bad report about Canaan which discourages many in Israel. [14]**Israel rebel** against Moses and complain against God. Caleb and Joshua (two faithful Israelites) tell the people not to rebel, and God says that the complainers won't enter Canaan, but only their children will. God also says that they will spend **forty years in the wilderness** as punishment for their rebellion.

[15]God tells Moses laws about sacrifices. [16]A son of Levi called Korah gets a group of men together, and they rebel against Moses, accusing him of exalting himself over Israel unfairly. God destroys Korah and the group of rebels. [17]God reaffirms his choice of Aaron as the head of the priestly line, and [18]outlines the duties of the Priests and the Levites, and [19]the laws about cleanliness. [20]The people of Israel complain about a water shortage, so God tells Moses to tell a rock to give out water, but instead Moses strikes the rock and it pours out water. God is angry with Moses for breaking faith with Him. Israel asks Edom if they can pass through their land, but Edom refuses. Aaron dies.

[21]Israel gets impatient and complains against God. God sends snakes that bite many, and God tells Moses to make a bronze serpent so that anyone who looks at it won't perish. Israel continues to be victorious in battle and steadfast in travelling, and they [22]camp in the plains of Moab. The king of Moab, **Balak**, fears that Israel will destroy Moab, so He calls upon **Balaam** – a man renowned for the ability to pronounce blessings and curses – to curse Israel. God speaks to Balaam and tells him that Israel is blessed, and therefore Balaam doesn't curse Israel, so [23-24]Balak grows angry. [25]Israel joins Moab in Baal worship, and God is angry. A son of Aaron, Phinehas, kills one of his fellow Israelites for bringing a Midianite woman into his family. God is pleased with Phinehas and establishes a covenant of peace and perpetual priesthood with him. [26]God tells Moses to conduct a census of all of Israel.

[27]God tells Moses that he will die before entering Canaan, and that **Joshua** (a faithful Israelite) will be the new leader for Israel. [28-29]God tells Moses about the rules for offerings and [30]making vows, and [31]tells him to gather men to make war with the Midianites to avenge the people of

Israel. [32]The tribes of Reuben and Gad see land outside Canaan that is good for livestock, so they ask Moses if they can have it, and not cross over the Jordan. God is angry at them for not following Him wholeheartedly, but allows them to have the land on the condition that they cross over the Jordan to encourage the rest of Israel first.

[33]Israel's geographical journey is recounted, and God tells Israel to drive out the inhabitants of Canaan when they enter it. [34]The boundaries of Canaan are defined and tribal chiefs are chosen. [35]God tells Israel to give the Levites some of the inheritance, and He explains what 'cities of refuge' are. [36]God reaffirms that no inheritance shall be transferred from one tribe to another. The Israelites continue to camp in the plains of Moab by the Jordan at Jericho.

Deuteronomy

[1]Israel's previous refusal to enter Canaan is recounted, as well as [2]their previous wandering in the wilderness. [3]Israel's battle victories are recounted. God reminds Moses that Joshua will lead the people into Canaan.

[4]**Moses commands Israel to obey God** with all their hearts. [5]He recounts the Ten Commandments, and [6]the greatest commandment: to love God with all your heart, soul and might. [7]Moses reminds Israel of the God's sovereignty in choosing Israel as His people, and thus Israel can trust God to let them enter and possess Canaan. [8]Moses tells Israel to guard against pride and to remember God when they enter Canaan. [9]Moses reminds Israel that it is not because of their righteousness that God is giving them Canaan. Rather, it is because of the wickedness of the gentile nations, and because of the promises that God has made to Abraham, Isaac and Jacob.

[10-11]Moses exhorts Israel to fear God, to walk in His ways, to love Him, and to serve Him. [12-13]Moses reminds Israel of some key statutes that God has set out: to worship God alone, to flee from idolatry, and to offer sacrifices in a way that honours God. [14]Moses reminds Israel about clean and unclean foods, laws about tithing, [15]the Sabbath year, [16]the Passover, the Feast of Weeks and the Feast of Booths. [17]Moses again warns against idolatry. God reveals that when Israel enters Canaan, if they want to, they can set a king over themselves. The qualifications for kingship are explained. [18]God promises to send a prophet like Moses to

speak to Israel on God's behalf. This promise speaks of Jesus (See Acts 3:22-24).

[19]Moses reminds Israel about Cities of Refuge. [20]He tells Israel laws concerning warfare, [21]unsolved murders, captives of war, rebellious children, the curse of being hung on a tree, [22]sexual immorality, [23]exclusion from the congregation, [24]divorce, [25]marriage, justice, [26]tithing and the giving of Firstfruits. [27]Moses commands Israel to make an altar on Mount Ebal when they cross over the Jordan, and to write the words of the law on the altar. [28]He outlines curses for sins and blessings for obedience. [29]God renews his **covenant** with Israel, and warns the people that they will be cursed if they disobey. [30]Moses calls Israel to repentance, because only then will God restore their fortunes.

[31]Moses gives the written law to the priests, and tells them to read it to the whole congregation of Israel after every seven years. God tells Moses that he will die soon, and that Joshua will take over Moses as the leader of Israel. God reveals to Moses that after Israel enters Canaan, they will rebel, and many troubles will come upon them. God reveals that He knows what Israel are inclined to do, and what they will do. [32]Moses speaks a song to all the congregation of Israel concerning God's faithfulness in guiding Israel, God's justice in dealing with Israel's sin, and God's love in showing mercy to His people. God tells Moses that he will die soon, and he will not enter Canaan (although he will see it), because Moses broke faith with God at the waters of the wilderness of Zin (See Numbers   20).

[33]Moses speaks his final blessing to Israel. [34]He goes up a mountain and sees all of Canaan, and **he dies.** The people of Israel start obeying and **following Joshua**, as God commanded them to do.

Joshua

[1]God tells Joshua to cross the Jordan with Israel. God promises that **Israel will inherit Canaan**. God tells Joshua to be strong and courageous; to obey the law and meditate on it day and night. [2]Joshua sends two spies into Canaan. They enter the house of a prostitute named **Rahab**. The king of Jericho sends men to find the spies, but Rahab hides them. She expresses her faith in the God of Israel, and asks the spies to spare her and her household when Israel enters Canaan. The spies agree to this, and they go back to Joshua and tell him all that had happened.

[3]**Israel crosses the Jordan**, and [4]Joshua sets up twelve memorial stones at Gilgal, to remind Israel that God let them cross the Jordan safely. [5]Joshua circumcises all the sons of Israel. Israel celebrates the Passover. Joshua sees a man with a drawn sword, who turns out to be the commander of the army of the Lord. [6]Israel marches around the city of Jericho and captures it. Rahab the prostitute and all her family are saved. [7]An Israelite called Achan steals some plundered items that were supposed to be devoted to destruction, so God becomes angry with the people of Israel. Achan's sin is exposed and he is stoned to death, and God turns from His burning anger.

[8]God tells Joshua to go to the city of Ai and defeat it. Joshua and all the fighting men use ambush tactics to defeat the people of Ai. Joshua builds an altar to God on Mount Ebal (in obedience to Deuteronomy 27). Joshua reads the words of the law to all Israel. [9]The Gibeonites trick Israel into making a peace covenant with them by telling Israel that they

are not inhabitants of Canaan. When Joshua finds out who they really are, he decides to make them servants for Israel. [10]Five Amorite kings make war with Gibeon and Israel, and Israel defeats them in battle. [11]More kings come to make war with Israel, but **Israel defeats them all and takes their lands**. [12]The kings that were defeated in Moses' time are outlined, and the kings that were defeated in Joshua's time are outlined.

[13]The remaining land yet to be conquered is outlined. The **allotments of land** given to the tribes of Reuben, Gad, Manasseh, and Levi are outlined. [14]Joshua allots land to Caleb (in fulfilment of the promise made to him in Deuteronomy 1:36). [15]Land allotments are outlined for Judah, [16]Ephraim, [17]Manasseh, [18]Benjamin, [19]Simeon, Zebulun, Issachar, Asher, Naphtali, Dan, and Joshua. [20]Israel sets apart the Cities of Refuge and [21]gives the Levites some cities and pasturelands. [22]The people of Reuben, Gad and Manasseh build an altar to God to be a lasting reminder that they are the Lord's people. The rest of Israel misunderstand the altar and think that they are rebelling against God, so they go to make war with them. Reuben, Gad and Manasseh explain why they built the altar, and everyone is happy. [23]Joshua brings together all Israel and charges them to cling to the Lord their God. [24]Israel makes a covenant, promising that they will put away false Gods and fear the true God in sincerity and faithfulness. Joshua dies.

Judges

^{1}Israel continues to take over Canaan. However, as Israel grows stronger they do not drive out the Canaanites completely but instead put them to forced labour. ^{2}The people of Israel start to worship the Baals, and God allows them to be harmed in battle. **God raises up judges to point Israel to God, but Israel doesn't listen to them, so God is angry with Israel.**

^{3}God sends judges called Othniel, Ehud, and Shamgar to save Israel. ^{4}A prophetess named **Deborah** becomes a judge in Israel, and she tells an Israelite called Barak to fight against the oppressive king of Canaan. So Barak gathers men and makes war, and God gives him victory over the king of Canaan. ^{5}Deborah and Balak sing a victory song of thanks to God.

^{6}Israel sins against God, and Midian starts to dominate them in battle. God tells a man called **Gideon** to destroy Israel's Baal worship and to fight against Midian. ^{7}Gideon gets three hundred men and makes war with Midian. ^{8}They defeat Midian and make an ornament out of the gold they plunder, and the people of Israel whore after it. Gideon dies. Israel again worships the Baals.

^{9}Abimelech – one of Gideon's sons – kills his seventy brothers in order to become ruler in Shechem. He continues to kill people to retain his rule, but he's eventually killed. ^{10}Two men – Tola and Jair – judge Israel, but they die. Israel sins against God and God is angry with them. The Ammonites come to fight Israel, but Israel has no ruler to save them.

[11]A warrior from Gilead called **Jephthah** is elected leader of Israel, and God gives him victory in battle against the Ammonites. Sadly, he makes a vow which forces him to sacrifice his own daughter. [12]Ephraim attacks Jephthah and Gilead because Jephthah didn't ask for Ephraim's help in battle. Gilead wins, establishing territory against Ephraim. Jephthah dies.

Three more judges – Ibzan, Elon and Abdon – judge Israel; and they die. [13]Israel sins against God and God gives them up to the Philistines. The Angel of the Lord appears to a man called Manoah and tells him that he will have a son who will save Israel from the Philistines. Manoah's wife gives birth to **Samson**.

[14]Samson marries a Philistine woman, because God was seeking an opportunity against the Philistines. [15]Samson's wife and father-in-law are killed by the Philistines, and he kills many Philistines in battle. [16]He loves a Philistine woman called Delilah, and Philistine leaders tell Delilah to find out where Samson's strength lies. Samson reveals that his strength lies in his hair. His hair is cut off and he's put in prison. He's made to entertain the Philistines at a house party. He prays to God and is enabled to push down the pillars of the house, killing the Philistines and himself.

[17]**Micah**, a man from Ephraim, makes for himself a shrine and household Gods, and he invites a travelling Levite to become a priest in his house. Israel has no king and everyone is doing what they want. [18]The tribe of Dan is without land, so they wander into the region of Ephraim. The tribe of Dan steals Micah's household gods, and makes the Levite (whose name is revealed to be Jonathan) a priest over the tribe of Dan. The tribe of Dan leaves Ephraim, takes over a small village and establishes a land for themselves.

[19]A Levite from Ephraim takes for himself a concubine, but she runs away and goes to her father's house in Bethlehem. But the Levite goes after her, and wins her back, and they start to journey back to Ephraim. However, they stay one night in **Gibeah** – a place belonging to the tribe of Benjamin – and the men of the city rape and abuse the concubine, and she dies. The Levite cuts her into twelve pieces and sends her throughout all the territories of Israel. [20]In reaction to the evil committed by Gibeah, the other tribes defeat them in battle. [21]The people of Israel show compassion to the tribe of Benjamin, and proclaim peace to them. The people of Israel attack Jabesh-gilead because they didn't aid Israel in battle, and Israel gives the surviving women from Jabesh-gilead to the tribe of Benjamin to be wives. Everyone goes back to their homes, and **Israel is still without a king.**

Ruth

[1]A woman from Bethlehem named **Naomi** has two daughters-in-law that she has to look after. Naomi tells the two to leave her; to go back to their parents' houses, and remarry there. One daughter-in-law leaves, but the other, named **Ruth**, stays with Naomi. The two go to Bethlehem.

[2]Ruth meets one of Naomi's relatives – a man called **Boaz** – and he lets her gather food from his field for the harvest season. [3]Naomi sends Ruth to go and sleep at Boaz's feet. Ruth does this, and Boaz awakes, and Ruth requests that he would redeem her. Boaz says that there is a closer redeemer than himself (i.e. a closer relative; see Leviticus 25:48-49), but if that person won't redeem her, then he will. [4]Boaz meets with Ruth's closest eligible redeemer and they hand over redeeming rights to Boaz. So **Boaz redeems Ruth**, marries her, and they have a child called Obed. Obed becomes the father of Jesse, who becomes the father of **David**.

1 Samuel

[1]A man from Ephraim called Elkanah has two wives: Hannah, who is barren, and Peninnah, who isn't. Hannah vows that if God gives her a son, then she will give him to God. God allows Hannah to give birth to Samuel. [2]Hannah thanks God.

Samuel ministers to God in the sight of a priest named Eli. God speaks to Eli, saying that He will destroy his children because of their wickedness, and He will establish a faithful priest who shall minister before God's anointed forever. [3]God tells Samuel the same thing, and **Samuel is established as a Prophet in Israel**.

[4]Israel, armed with the Ark of the Covenant, goes out to battle against the Philistines. **The Philistines defeat Israel and capture the Ark of the Covenant**. Eli's two sons die in battle. Eli is told of Israel's defeat, and in shock he falls backwards, breaks his neck and dies. [5]The Philistines bring the Ark to Ashdod, but God afflicts the people of Ashdod. They move the Ark around Philistia, but God keeps afflicting the Philistines. So they decide to send the Ark back to Israel. [6]**The Philistines return the Ark and** [7]**Samuel tells Israel to put away all their foreign gods and serve God alone.** Israel agrees and goes to Mizpah to confess their sins to God. The Philistines come to attack them, but Israel defeats them in battle.

[8]Israel sees that Samuel is getting old and that his sons are wicked, so they ask Samuel to appoint a king to judge Israel like all the other nations, and God tells Samuel to obey their request. Samuel warns them

about having a king, but Israel doesn't listen to him – **they demand a king to judge them.** [9]A man from Benjamin called Kish has a son called Saul. Kish loses his donkeys, so he gets Saul to go and look for them. Saul goes, and in need of help he goes to Ephraim because he knows Samuel is a prophet who can help him find the donkeys. However, Samuel had received a word from God telling him to make Saul prince over Israel. [10]**Samuel brings all Israel together and makes Saul king over Israel.**

[11]The Ammonites threaten to fight and disgrace Jabesh-gilead, so Saul gathers many Israelites to defend Jabesh-gilead, and they defeat the Ammonites in battle. [12]Samuel gives a farewell address to Israel. He recounts the goodness that God has shown to Israel, and he recounts the wickedness shown by Israel. He tells Israel that, although they had sinned in asking for a king, they should still serve God faithfully.

[13]Saul's army, including his son Jonathan, fight against the Philistines. Saul hides with his men in Gilgal and offers sacrifices to God impatiently, ignoring Samuel's instructions to wait (10:8). Samuel says that Saul's kingdom will not last. [14]Jonathan valiantly kills many Philistines in battle, and God saves Israel from the Philistines. Saul makes a rash oath that forces people not to eat food. This makes many Israelites faint, and almost costs Jonathan his life. [15]God tells Saul to destroy the Amalekites, so Saul attacks the Amalekites, but he disobeys God by sparing the king and the best animals. **God regrets making Saul king, and He rejects Saul so that he is no longer king.**

[16]God sends Samuel to a man in Bethlehem called Jesse. **Samuel anoints Jesse's youngest son David, and makes him king.** A harmful spirit enters

Saul, and his servants suggest he find a lyre player to put the harmful spirit at ease. Saul hires David to play the lyre.

[17]The Philistines gather to battle against Israel. A Philistine champion called Goliath taunts the Israelites, demanding a one-on-one fight. **David fights Goliath and defeats him.** The Philistines flee and Israel is victorious. [18]David and Jonathan become good friends. David marries Saul's daughter Michal. His success over the Philistines continues, and **Saul becomes jealous of David.** [19]**He tries to kill David, but David flees** to Naioth. [20]David visits Jonathan, who warns him that Saul wants to kill him. [21]David deceives a Priest in Nob and a King in Gath in order to flee from Saul [22]to Judah. Saul, hearing that David had been in Nob, goes to Nob and kills every living thing there.

[23]Saul continues to pursue David. [24]He inadvertently enters a cave where David and his men are hiding. David doesn't attack Saul, but spares his life. Saul leaves the cave and David follows him and tells him that he'd spared his life. Saul responds thankfully and wishes good upon David.

[25]Samuel dies. David sends messengers to Carmel to ask a man called Nabal for some supplies, but Nabal refuses them. David and his men go to attack the men of Carmel, but Nabal's wife Abigail pleads for forgiveness. David spares their lives, and God kills Nabal soon after. Abigail becomes David's wife, along with another woman.

[26]Saul and his army go out to kill David again. While the army is asleep, David has another chance to kill Saul and he spares his life again. When Saul realises this, he confesses his sin and blesses David. [27]David doesn't trust Saul and flees to Philistia. [28]The Philistines prepare to make war

with Israel. Saul goes to a medium for guidance. Through the medium, Saul talks to Samuel, who tells him that God will tear the kingdom out of his hand and give it to David. [29]The Philistine leaders see that David is among their ranks on the way to battle Israel, and for fear of him attacking them, they send him back to the lands of Philistia. [30]David goes to Ziklag – a part of Israel which the Amalekites had attacked. David and his men go after the Amalekites and strike them down.

[31]**The Philistines attack Israel. Saul and his sons, including Jonathan, are all killed.**

2 Samuel

[1]David weeps when he hears about the deaths of Saul and his sons. [2]David is appointed king over Judah, while Ish-bosheth (a relative of Saul) is appointed king over the rest of Israel. The two men's armies come together and fight. [3]Ishbosheth insults one of his men – Abner, a former commander of Saul's army – so he joins David and makes him king over all Israel. Joab – the commander of David's army – suspects Abner of deceit, so he kills him. However, David rebukes Joab for his sin, and mourns the death of Abner. [4]Ish-bosheth is betrayed and murdered by two of his own men.

[5]**David is anointed king over Israel. He captures Jerusalem and sets it up to serve as the stronghold city of Israel. He defeats the Philistines in battle. He becomes greater and greater because God is with him.** [6]David brings the Ark of God to Jerusalem. Sadly, a man called Uzzah touches the Ark and dies. One of David's wives, Michal, despises David for dancing with joy besides the Ark.

[7]**God promises to make for David a great name and an everlasting kingdom. God promises to raise up David's offspring, who will build a house for God's name, and who will be a son to God.** David praises God for His faithfulness and greatness. [8]God gives David victory in battle against Philistia, Moab, Assyria, Edom and others. [9]David shows kindness to a crippled son of Jonathan called Mephibosheth, and lets him eat at his table. [10]David defeats the Syrians and Ammonites in battle.

[11]David stays in Jerusalem while his army goes to battle. **He sleeps with a woman called Bathsheba** – the wife of a warrior called Uriah – and she becomes pregnant. David covers up his sin by putting Uriah in the frontline of battle, so that Uriah dies. [12]God sends a prophet called Nathan to rebuke David for his sin. Bathsheba gives birth, but the child dies, and God says that David's wives will be given to one of his neighbours. **David confesses his sin, and Bathsheba gives birth to Solomon.** God gives David victory in battle against the Ammonites.

[13]One of David's sons named Amnon rapes his own sister. Another son of David, Absalom, murders Amnon out of anger and then flees. [14]Joab convinces David to allow Absalom to return to Jerusalem. **Absalom returns [15]and deceptively wins over the people of Israel, making himself king.** David and his staff flee the city of Jerusalem to escape Absalom and his supporters. [16]Whilst fleeing towards the Jordan, David is met by a servant of Mephibosheth called Ziba, who gives him food and supplies. He is also met by a relative of Saul called Shimei, who curses him. Absalom enters Jerusalem and sleeps with David's concubines in the sight of Israel. [17]An adviser to Absalom called Ahithophel tells Absalom to go out and attack David. A friend of David called Hushai is called by Absalom to give a second opinion, and he tells Absalom to wait a bit longer before attacking David. Absalom follows Hushai's advice, and therefore David is saved. David and his people cross the Jordan and continue fleeing, but Absalom and his army follow soon after. [18]Absalom's army battles against David's army, and **Absalom is killed and defeated by David's army.** When David hears of Absalom's death he weeps, because he loved him. [19]Joab, commander of David's army, rebukes David for mourning over his rival Absalom. David crosses the

Jordan and returns to Jerusalem. He pardons those who he suspected to be enemies during Absalom's reign.

[20]A man called Sheba stirs up a rebellion against David, so David's army pursues and kills Sheba. [21]Israel experiences famine because of past sin that Saul had committed against the Gibeonites. David appeases the Gibeonites by giving them seven of Saul's sons to be hung. Israel defeats the Philistines in battle. [22]David sings a song of thankfulness to God for being His refuge and salvation. [23]He speaks his last words; he talks about God's faithfulness and justice. David's closest military companions are outlined. [24]David takes a census of Israel. He acknowledges his sinfulness and asks God for mercy. God sends a plague on Israel, but it subsides when David builds an altar to God.

1 Kings

[1]David grows old and a man called Adonijah tries to set himself up as king, but **David hands the kingship over to Solomon**. [2]David dies.

Solomon sends a servant called Benaiah to kill Adonijah, Joab (who was disloyal to David as army commander), and Shimei (because he disobeyed Solomon and left Jerusalem). Solomon makes Benaiah the new commander of his army. Solomon's kingship is firmly established.

[3]**Solomon asks God for wisdom, and God gives him it.** He judges a case involving two women claiming ownership of a child. [4]His staff, wealth, and wisdom are all outlined.

[5]The king of Tyre, called Hiram, helps Solomon to prepare to build the Temple of God. [6]**Solomon builds the Temple** [7]**and his own palace.** [8]The Ark of the Covenant is brought into the Temple and Solomon blesses all of Israel, calling them to obey God and love him in their hearts and minds. He prays to God for justice and mercy for all who pray faithfully towards the Temple. [9]God speaks to Solomon, and tells him that if he obeys God's word, God will preserve Israel, but if he disobeys, God will cut off Israel from the land of Canaan and the Temple will be destroyed.

[10]The Queen of Sheba visits Solomon and is impressed by his wisdom. She gives many gifts to him, and he supplies her with gifts in return. Solomon, excelling in wealth, builds many things using fine gold.

[11]Solomon's **many foreign wives** turn away his heart from serving God, and he serves **false Gods**. God is angry with Solomon and raises up adversaries against him. God says that He will tear the kingdom away from Solomon, and will give ten tribes to one of his servants, Jeroboam. **Solomon dies, and one of his sons, Rehoboam, reigns in his place in Jerusalem.**

[12]**The kingdom is divided. The people of Judah follow the house of David and institute Rehoboam as their king, but the rest of Israel institute Jeroboam as their king.** Jeroboam, not wanting his people to have to travel to Jerusalem in Judah to offer sacrifices at the Temple, makes two golden calves and presents them as Gods for the people of Israel. [13]A prophet from Judah tells Jeroboam that a man from the house of David called Josiah will one day demolish Jeroboam's priests. The man of God, journeying back to Judah, disobeys God's order not to eat bread in the land, and is eaten by a lion. Jeroboam continues his evil practices. [14]Jeroboam's wife goes to a prophet called Ahijah, who tells her that because of Jeroboam's sinfulness, Israel will be uprooted and scattered. Jeroboam dies, and his son, Nadab, reigns in his place. Rehoboam also does evil in the sight of God. The king of Egypt comes and attacks Jerusalem, removing its gold that Solomon had made. Rehoboam dies, and his son, Abijam, reigns in his place.

[15]Abijam rules in Judah, does evil in God's sight, and dies. His son, Asa, takes his place, does right in God's sight, and dies. His son, Jehoshaphat, reigns in his place.

Nadab reigns in Israel, but a man from Issachar called Baasha kills him along with all of Jeroboam's family, and reigns in his place. [16]Baasha reigns in Israel, does evil, and dies. His son Elah reigns in his place, but a servant called Zimri kills him and reigns in his place. Zimri is killed by the commander of Israel's army, named Omri, who reigns in his place. Omri dies, and his son **Ahab** reigns in his place. Ahab worships Baal and Asherah, and his wife Jezebel kills many prophets of Yahweh.

[17]A man from Gilead called **Elijah** goes to Ahab and tells him that **it won't rain in Israel** for a time, according to God's will. God directs Elijah to a brook for water, and then to a widow where he receives food and drink. Elijah prays for the widow's dead son, and God revives the boy. [18]Elijah tells Ahab to gather **the prophets of Baal at Mount Carmel**. Elijah and the false prophets gather, each with a bull, to see who can pray to God to consume their bull with fire. The prophets of Baal fail, while Elijah's prayers are answered by God with fire upon his bull. Elijah slaughters the prophets of Baal after his victory. God sends rain; the famine/drought ends.

[19]Elijah flees from Israelites who have forsaken God's covenant and have turned to serve other Gods. God speaks to him in a low whisper at Mount Horeb and tells him to anoint a man called Hazael to be king over Syria, a man called Jehu to be king over Israel, and a man called **Elisha** to be prophet alongside Elijah. [20]Syria fights against Israel twice and Israel defeats them both times. However, God told Ahab to devote all the Syrian army to destruction, but he spared their king, so a prophet prophesies Ahab's death.

[21]A man called Naboth has a vineyard, and Ahab asks him if he can buy it, but Naboth won't sell it. Ahab's wife Jezebel has Naboth killed, and Ahab takes possession of the vineyard. God sends Elijah to tell Ahab that God

will destroy him. However, Ahab repents and humbles himself in sorrow, so God relents and promises to bring disaster not on Ahab, but on his sons. ²²Ahab goes to fight the Syrians, and he dies, and Ahaziah reigns in his place and continues to do evil. Jehoshaphat, king of Judah, dies, and his son Jehoram reigns in his place.

2 Kings

¹Elijah prophesies Ahaziah's death. Ahaziah dies and a man called Jehoram reigns in his place.

²Elijah and Elisha cross the Jordan and **Elijah is taken up to heaven by God in a whirlwind. Elisha is given a double portion of Elijah's spirit.** He purifies a town's water and summons two bears to devour some boys that were mocking him. ³The king of Moab rebels against Israel, so Jehoram king of Israel teams up with Jehoshaphat king of Judah, and they go to attack Moab. They lack water on the way, but Elisha tells them that God will supply them with water and will allow them to devastate the land of Moab. God gives them water, and they attack Moab and devastate the land, but after a while they're forced to retreat and return home.

⁴Elisha miraculously helps a widow with her debt; God supplies her with much oil to sell. A woman generously provides Elisha with food and a small room to stay in, so he tells her that she will have a son, and God gives her a son. The son later dies, but Elisha raises it to life. Elisha purifies a deadly stew at a meal and feeds a hundred men with twenty loaves of barley. ⁵He heals Naaman, the commander of the Syrian army, of leprosy. Elisha's servant, Gehazi, extorts a reward from Naaman, so the leprosy is put on Gehazi. ⁶Elisha miraculously recovers an axe head from a river.

He helps the king of Israel predict **Syrian attacks**, so the Syrians go to capture Elisha, but he is surrounded by ally horses and chariots that only he can see, and he blinds the Syrians and takes them to Samaria. In Samaria, the Syrians are fed and let go, never to raid Israel again, but they return and attack Samaria. A great famine begins in Samaria, but [7]Elisha says that God will supply Israel with food. God makes the Syrians hear sounds of chariots, so the Syrians flee their city. Israel goes into Syria and eats their food, ending the famine.

[8]The king of Syria, Ben-hadad, is murdered by one of his servants, called Hazael, who reigns in his place. Jehoram does evil and dies, and his son, Ahaziah, reigns in his place, and does evil. Edom revolts against Judah and sets up a king for themselves. [9]Elisha sends a messenger to an army commander called Jehu, who is anointed king over Israel and told to strike down the house of Ahab. Jehu goes to Joram/Jehoram, king of Israel, and kills him, and reigns in his place. [10]Jehu kills the remaining sons of Ahab, according to God's word spoken through Elijah. Jehu cunningly gathers and kills all the Baal-worshipers, thus wiping out Baal worship from Israel. Jehu dies, and his son Jehoahaz reigns in his place.

[11]Ahaziah king of Judah dies, and his mother, Athaliah, reigns in his place. However, a priest named Jehoiada commands army captains to anoint one of Athaliah's sons named Joash king, and they do so, and Athaliah is put to death. Joash removes Baal worship from Judah. [12]He raises money and hires people to repair the Temple of the Lord. Hazael, king of Syria, goes to attack Jerusalem, but Joash gives him all the gold from the treasuries of the Temple, so he goes away. Joash is killed by his servants, and Amaziah his son reigns in his place.

[13]Jehoahaz king of Israel does evil, and Israel is oppressed by Syria. Jehoahaz dies, and his son, Joash, reigns in his place. Joash does evil and dies, and his son, Jeroboam, reigns in his place. Elisha becomes ill, and Joash visits him, and Elisha tells him that he will defeat Syria three times. The king of Syria, Hazael, dies, and his son, Ben-hadad, reigns in his place, and is defeated by Joash three times.

[14]Amaziah defeats many Edomites and challenges Joash king of Israel to a battle. Amaziah / Judah is defeated by Joash / Israel. Amaziah dies and his son Azariah reigns in his place. Joash dies and his son Jeroboam reigns in his place. Jeroboam dies, and his son Zechariah reigns in his place. [15]Azariah dies, and Jotham his son reigns in his place. Zechariah is killed by a man called Shallum, who reigns in his place, but is killed by a man called Menahem, who reigns in his place, but is killed by Pekahiah, who reigns in his place, but is killed by a man called Pekah, who reigns in his place. Assyria begins to capture parts of Israel. Jotham dies and Ahaz reigns in his place.

[16]Syria and Israel attack Judah and do some damage. Ahaz dies and his son Hezekiah reigns in his place. [17]A man called Hoshea begins to reign in Israel. **The king of Assyria attacks and defeats Israel, and takes them into exile.** The author explains that Israel was exiled because of their rejection of God. Samaria is repopulated by Assyrians who don't fear God.

[18]**Hezekiah** reigns over Judah, and does good. The king of Assyria comes to Judah, and Hezekiah sends messengers out to him. The king of Assyria tells them to distrust God and ignore Hezekiah, but the messengers refuse and remain faithful to God and return back to Hezekiah. [19]A

prophet named Isaiah tells Hezekiah to continue to trust in God, and says that God will protect Judah against Assyria. Hezekiah prays for salvation, and God strikes down many Assyrians and the king goes home to Assyria. Later, the king of Assyria is killed by his sons. [20]Hezekiah falls ill, so he prays that God would heal him, and God does so. Isaiah says that Judah will be exiled to Babylon. Hezekiah dies, and his son **Manasseh** reigns in his place.

[21]Manasseh does much evil as king, and God says that Judah will be given into the hands of their enemies. Manasseh dies and his son Amon becomes king, does evil and dies, and his son **Josiah** becomes king.

[22]Josiah does good, and he makes arrangements to repair the Temple. One of his messengers finds the book of the law, which was previously lost in the temple. Josiah's messengers go to a prophetess who tells them that God will bring disaster upon Judah. [23]Josiah reads the words of God's law in the presence of all of Judah, and they make a covenant of obedience to God. Josiah removes idol worship from Judah, and he restores the Passover. He dies while battling the king of Egypt. His son Jehoahaz reigns in his place, but he is removed by the Pharaoh of Egypt, who puts Jehoiakim, another son of Josiah, as king over Judah.

[24]Jehoiakim does evil and dies, and his son Jehoiachin reigns in his place. Nebuchadnezzar king of Babylon starts to take Jerusalem into exile, and he makes Jehoiachin's uncle Zedekiah king in Judah. [25]**Nebuchadnezzar king of Babylon comes to Judah with his army. They demolish Judah: the land, the king's house, and the Temple. They capture the people of Judah and take them into exile in Babylon.**

1 Chronicles

[1]The descendents from Adam to Abraham to Jacob are outlined. [2]The genealogy of David is outlined. [3]The descendents of: David, [4]Judah, Simeon, [5]Reuben, Gad, the members of the half-tribe of Manasseh, [6]Levi, [7]Issachar, Benjamin, Naphtali, Manasseh, Ephraim and Asher are outlined. [8]The genealogy of Saul is outlined. [9]The exiles from Israel and Judah who have returned and resettled in Israel are outlined. [10]The death of Saul and his sons is recounted.

[11]**David is anointed king.** He captures Jerusalem to serve as Israel's capital. His mighty men (his closest army friends) are outlined. [12]Warriors from all over Israel come to join David's army, to establish him as king over Israel. [13]David gathers Israel to bring the ark to Jerusalem. A man called Uzzah touches the ark, and God kills him, so David decides to send the ark to the household of a man called Obed-edom for safe keeping. [14]The Philistines try to attack Israel, but David and his army defeat them. [15]He gathers Israel to bring the ark from Obed-Edom's house to Jerusalem, and they do so. [16]He brings the ark into a tent he had pitched, and he appoints Levites to minister before the ark. All of Israel sings praise to God, thanking Him for His awesome works.

[17]**God makes a covenant with David.** He promises to build a house for David and to plant Israel in safety, and He promises to establish a descendent of David as king forever. David thanks God.

[18]David defeats many enemy nations in battle. [19]The king of the Ammonites dies, so David sends messengers to console the king's son. However, the king's son mistreats the messengers and joins the Syrians in making war against Israel. David defeats the Ammonites and the Syrians. [20]Israel attacks and defeats the Ammonites and the Philistines.

[21]Satan incites David to take a census of Israel, and he does so. God is angry with David and strikes Israel with pestilence. God tells David to build an altar for sacrifices, and he does so, and God relents from his anger and stops striking Israel.

[22]David makes preparations to build the temple for God. He hands the task over to his son Solomon, because Solomon was the one promised by God to accomplish the task. [23]**David makes Solomon king** over Israel. David organizes the Levites, who are to assist the sons of Aaron in the service of the Temple. [24]David organizes priests, [25]musicians, and [26]gatekeepers for service in the Temple. [27]He organizes the leaders of the military divisions and the tribal chiefs.

[28]David assembles all Israel and recounts the promises that God had made to him. He tells them to obey God wholeheartedly, and he tells Solomon to be strong in the Lord and to accomplish the work of building the Temple. [29]David calls upon Israel to offer wealth to go towards the building of the Temple, and people offer up wealth generously, and everyone rejoices. David humbly thanks God and prays that God would guide Israel in obedience, and guide Solomon in the construction of the temple. Israel anoints Solomon as king, and David dies.

2 Chronicles

[1]Solomon is king over Israel. God allows him to ask for anything, so Solomon asks for **wisdom** to govern Israel. God promises these to him, along with riches and honour.

[2]Solomon prepares to build the Temple by requesting supplies from the king of Tyre. [3-4]**Solomon builds the Temple.** [5]The ark is brought into the inner sanctuary of the temple, Israel gathers to celebrate and the glory of God fills the temple. [6]Solomon praises God for his faithfulness in fulfilling the promise made to David, that a Temple for the Lord would be built. Solomon prays for continued covenantal faithfulness; he asks that God would forgive Israel when they seek Him in prayer. [7]God answers Solomon and says that if Israel humbly seeks Him in prayer, He will forgive them of their sins and heal the land. Obedience will lead to blessing while disobedience will lead to disaster.

[8]Solomon continues to build up the land of Israel and organize the people in it. [9]The Queen of Sheba visits Solomon and praises him for his wisdom and wealth. **Solomon dies**, and his son Rehoboam reigns in his place. [10]The people of Israel ask Rehoboam to lighten the workload put on them by Solomon. Rehoboam rejects the council of old men, and listens to his friends, and tells Israel that he will increase the workload. **Judah follows Rehoboam, but Israel follows a man called Jeroboam.** [11]Rehoboam secures his reign over Judah and Benjamin. He has many wives and children. Priests and Levites come to serve under his rule.

[12]Rehoboam and all of Israel abandon God's law. The king of Egypt strikes Jerusalem, destroying much gold, but Israel humble themselves and Rehoboam continues to reign in good conditions. Rehoboam dies, and his son Abijah reigns in his place. [13]Abijah assembles an army to battle against Israel / Jeroboam. Abijah confirms that Judah has not forsaken God, so God gives Judah victory in battle over Israel. Jeroboam dies.

[14]Abijah dies, and his son **Asa** reigns in his place over Judah. He does what is good in the eyes of God. A massive Ethiopian army comes against Judah. Asa prays for help, and God gives Judah victory over the Ethiopians. [15]Asa courageously removes all the idols from Judah. He and all of Judah make a covenant to God, promising to seek Him with all their hearts and souls. [16]Baasha, king of Israel, attempts to restrict people entering or leaving Judah. Asa pays the king of Syria to attack Israel, so Baasha's plan is foiled. A prophet tells Asa that, because he trusted in the Syrians rather than God, there will be wars in Judah from now on. Asa dies.

[17]Asa's son **Jehoshaphat begins to reign in Judah**. He seeks God and walks in His commandments, and he sends out officials to teach the book of the law of God throughout all Judah. God establishes his kingdom, and his armies grow. [18]Ahab king of Israel asks Jehoshaphat to join him as an ally in battle at Ramoth-gilead. Jehoshaphat agrees, but asks for prophets to seek God's advice. Hundreds of prophets tell them to go to war, but one prophet tells them that God has decreed disaster for them. They go to war anyway, and Ahab dies in battle. [19]Jehoshaphat returns to Jerusalem, and he appoints judges to decide disputed cases in Judah. [20]A great army of Ammonites and Moabites come to attack Judah, so Judah

assembles and prays to God for rescue. God makes the enemy armies turn on one another, thus rescuing Judah from destruction. Jehoshaphat later joins Ahaziah king of Israel in building unauthorized ships for trade.

[21]Jehoshaphat dies, and his son Jehoram reigns in his place. He leads Judah away from seeking God. Edom revolts against Judah and sets up their own king. God stirs up the anger of the Philistines, and they invade Judah and take away many possessions. God strikes Jehoram with a bowel disease, and he dies.

[22]Jehoram's son Ahaziah becomes king in Judah. He does evil in God's sight. He goes to Israel to visit a son of Ahab named Joram. Upon visiting, he is killed by a man called Jehu (See 2 Kings chapters 8-10). Ahaziah's mother Athaliah begins to kill off the royal family in Judah, however one of Ahaziah's sons named Joash is hidden, and he survives. Athaliah begins to reign in Judah. [23]A priest called Jehoiada conspires with the rest of Judah to rebel against Athaliah. They set up Joash as king, and they kill Athaliah. They make a covenant with God to worship Him alone.

[24]Joash reigns in Judah with the assistance of Jehoiada the priest. Jehoiada grows old and dies, and the people of Judah start worshipping idols. Zechariah – a son of Jehoiada – speaks a prophecy against Judah, so the people of Judah, along with Joash, kill Zechariah. The Syrians attack Judah and wound Joash, and his servants conspire against him and kill him. His son Amaziah reigns in his place.

[25]Amaziah reigns in Judah, and he fights a battle without the assistance of Israel, so Israel becomes angry. Amaziah leads Judah in the worship of foreign gods, and he rejects the council of a prophet. He challenges the

king of Israel to a battle, and Judah defeats Israel in battle. The Jerusalem wall is broken down, and Amaziah dies.

[26]Amaziah's son Uzziah is made king in Judah. He is greatly helped by God: he builds up Judah structurally while maintaining a streak of military victories. He grows strong, but he also grows proud. He goes into the temple to burn incense, even though he's not supposed to. God strikes him with Leprosy, and he dies. His son Jotham reigns in his place.

[27]Jotham reigns in Judah, and he is greatly helped by God: he builds up Judah and enjoys military success. He dies, and his son Ahaz reigns in his place. [28]Ahaz reignites Baal worship and idolatry throughout Judah, so God gives Judah into the hands of Syria, Assyria, and Israel, who do great damage to the people of Judah. Ahaz dies and his son Hezekiah reigns in his place.

[29]**Hezekiah reigns in Judah,** and he repairs the temple and restores pure worship in Judah. [30]He sends messengers throughout Judah and Israel, trying to get everyone to come to Jerusalem to celebrate the Passover. Many people turn up not having consecrated themselves, but Hezekiah prays that God would pardon everyone despite them not adhering to the sanctuary's rules, and God does so. There is great joy in Judah. [31]Hezekiah continues to eradicate idol worship in Judah and Israel, and he organizes the priests in divisions. [32]The king of Assyria tries to invade Judah and sends messengers to Judah to blaspheme against God. Hezekiah prays to God for help and encourages Judah in their faith, and God defeats the Assyrian army for Judah. Hezekiah becomes sick and dies, and his son Manasseh reigns in his place.

[33]Manasseh reignites Baal worship and desecrates the Temple, so God sends the king of Assyria to exile him to Babylon. In exile, Manasseh humbles himself and prays for help. God answers and brings him back to Jerusalem, where he tries to restore pure worship. Manasseh dies, and his son Amnon reigns, does evil and dies, and his son Josiah reigns in his place.

[34]Josiah purges Judah of Baal worship. He funds workers to repair the temple. The workers find the book of the law (which was lost) in the temple. They bring it to Josiah, who reads it and weeps. God tells Josiah that he will destroy Judah because of its sinfulness. Josiah brings all of Judah together, reads the book of the law in their presence, and they enter into a covenant of obedience to God. [35]Judah celebrates the Passover. Josiah is killed by Egyptians in battle.

[36]Josiah's descendants – Jehoiakim, Jehoiachin and Zedekiah – reign in Judah and do evil, leading Judah astray. **King Nebuchadnezzar exiles all of Judah to Babylon.**

Once the kingdom of Persia is established in the place of Babylon, **Cyrus king of Persia is told by God to build him a house in Jerusalem.**

Ezra

[1]**God stirs up the spirit of Cyprus king of Persia so that he makes a decree for Israelite exiles to return to Jerusalem to rebuild the temple.** The exiles prepare for their return. [2]The returned exiles are outlined, and they prepare to rebuild the temple. [3]The altar is built and the temple foundations are laid. The people rejoice, but those who had seen the first temple weep.

[4]**Enemies of the rebuilding** frustrate the exiles' rebuilding progress, all throughout the reigns of Cyrus, Darius and Ahasuerus. During the reign of Artaxerxes, the enemies of Judah write a letter to Artaxerxes requesting that the exiles be made to stop building, and the request is granted. [5]The exiles resume rebuilding the temple without permission, and the enemies write a letter to Darius, the current king, asking him to search and see whether a decree was ever really made by Cyrus allowing the exiles to rebuild. [6]King Darius finds the decree set by Cyrus, allowing the exiles to rebuild, so he decrees for the enemies to keep away from the rebuilding, and to stop annoying the exiles. The exiles finish rebuilding the temple, and they celebrate the Passover.

[7]**Artaxerxes sends Ezra – a man trained in the law of God – to teach the exiles in Jerusalem.** More exiles come to Jerusalem with Ezra, bringing money to facilitate sacrifice and celebration, and more materials for rebuilding. [8]On the way to Jerusalem, Ezra spends time fasting and praying with the other exiles; seeking God's protection for their journey. They arrive at Jerusalem.

[9]The exiles intermarry with the peoples of the land and their abominations. Ezra weeps and prays to God, confessing the sin of the exiles. **[10]The whole of Israel confess their sins of intermarriage, and they make a covenant to God to put away their foreign wives and children.**

Nehemiah

[1]Nehemiah — the cupbearer to king Artaxerxes — hears of Jerusalem's brokenness; how its gates are demolished. Nehemiah confesses Israel's sin in prayer, and prays for success and mercy for himself. [2]Nehemiah asks the king to send him to Judah so he can repair it, and the king is pleased to do so. **Nehemiah goes to Jerusalem, inspects it, and invites the Israelites there to rebuild the wall with him.** [3]They begin to rebuild.

[4]**Opposition arises** as enemies taunt the exiles and plan to attack them. The exiles work with extra caution: half of them work on the wall while the other half guard the group with spears and swords. [5]Nehemiah stops the oppression of the poor; he stops people from exacting tax from those who are struggling financially. [6]Two men — Tobiah and Sanballat — conspire against Nehemiah and try to taunt him via letters. But Nehemiah doesn't fear them, and **the exiles finish building the wall**.

[7]The names of the returned exiles are outlined. [8]All the exiles gather, and **Ezra reads the words of the Law** to the whole assembly. All Israel rejoice that they were able to hear the word of the Law and understand it, and they celebrate the Feast of Booths. [9]**Nehemiah leads them in a prayer of confession**, and he recounts the story of how God saved Israel; how He brought them out of Egypt and gave them the land of Canaan, and remained faithful even when Israel was faithless. [10]The exiles enter into a **covenant** of obedience to God.

[11]The officials, [12]priests and Levites are outlined. All the exiles come together to celebrate the dedication of the Jerusalem wall. [13]Nehemiah deals with some problems in the community, such as Sabbath-breaking and intermarriage.

Esther

[1]King Ahasuerus – the king of Persia – holds a feast for everyone in Persia in order to show off his vast wealth and glory. During the feast, he asks his queen – Queen Vashti – to come out and show everyone how beautiful she is. Queen Vashti refuses to do so, and she is removed from her position as queen.

[2]**A Jewish exile named Mordecai has a beautiful cousin called Esther.** She is taken into the king's palace, along with other beautiful women, to try to please the king and win his favour. **The king loves Esther and makes her queen**, replacing Queen Vashti. Meanwhile, Mordecai foils a sinister plot against the king. [3]The king promotes a man in his service named **Haman**. Everyone pays homage to Haman except for Mordecai, and Haman is angry. He finds out that Mordecai is a Jew, and makes a decree for all Jews in Persia to be destroyed.

[4]Mordecai tells Esther what has happened, via a messenger. Mordecai asks Esther to go into King Ahasuerus's chamber – a risky procedure – to plead to him on the Jews' behalf. Esther complies. [5]She prepares a feast for the king and for Haman. She tells them that she will prepare another feast for them the next day, in which she will make a request to the king. Haman goes home joyful, but sees Mordecai not paying homage to him again, and is filled with rage. His friends tell him to hang Mordecai, and he is pleased with this idea.

[6]The king reads a book of memorable deeds, and learns that Mordecai had foiled a plot against him. Wanting to reward Mordecai, the king asks Haman what should be done to the person in whom the king delights. Haman, believing the question to be about him, says to dress the man in robes and proclaim in the city his favour. The king gets Haman to do this for Mordecai. Haman, humiliated, does this.

[7]The king and Haman come to the second feast prepared by Esther. She requests that the Jews stop being persecuted. The king realises that Haman was the one who requested their persecution, and so he hangs Haman, and grants Esther's request. **[8]The king honours Esther and Mordecai, and reverses Haman's decree, thus saving the Jews from persecution.** [9]The Jews in Persia attack those who were opposed to them, and destroy them. Mordecai inaugurates the Feast of Purim: a celebration of the Jewish liberation within Persia. [10]Mordecai sought peace and welfare for his people, and he succeeded.

OLD TESTAMENT

WISDOM

Job

[1]**Job** is a blameless, upright, wealthy man. **Satan** tells **God** that Job wouldn't be faithful if his possessions were taken away, so God grants Satan the power to destroy Job's livestock and children. Job remains faithful, accepting both the good and the bad from God. [2]God gives Satan the power to attack Job's health, so Satan strikes him with sores. Job's wife tells him to curse God and die, but he remains faithful. His three friends – Eliphaz, Bildad, and Zophar – come to comfort him. [3]He curses the day of his birth.

[4]**Eliphaz** tells Job that his suffering must be an indication of sinfulness. [5]He tells Job to seek God for mercy. [6]**Job** wants to die. He argues against his friends, saying they are no help, and he asserts his innocence. [7]He sees that life is so short and seemingly insignificant, and questions why God is punishing him.

[8]**Bildad** also tells Job that his suffering must be an indication of sinfulness. [9]**Job** asserts that God is greater than him, but he maintains his innocence. He longs for an arbiter between himself and God so that he would be able to ask God why he is suffering. [10]He wants to question God about his suffering. He loathes his life.

[11]**Zophar** answers and says that Job is wrong. Zophar asserts the unsearchable knowledge of God, and he calls Job to repent, saying that Job will only find peace and security when he repents. [12]**Job** points out that wicked men sometimes live their whole lives in peace and security.

He asserts the sovereignty, power and wisdom of God over his situation, but [13]he wants to argue his case with God. He despises his friends' bad advice. He still puts his trust in God, but he wants to know why God is letting him suffer. [14]Job sees that life is short, and wonders why it is full of troubles. He longs for his suffering to depart from him and for his sins to be covered. He supposes that God wears down the hope of man, and is against man, all the days of a man's life.

[15]**Eliphaz** says that Job is a sinner. [16]**Job** says that his friends are horrible comforters. [17]He questions whether he has any hope at all of being delivered from his anguish. [18]**Bildad** says that Job must be sinful. [19]**Job** says that even if he has sinned, his friends should still be better comforters. He looks forward to the day when he will see God. [20]**Zophar** describes the wrath experienced by the wicked, implying that Job is wicked. [21]**Job** points out that the wicked often prosper and live their lives in peace, from an Earthly perspective. He renounces the falsehood of his friends' comfort. [22]**Eliphaz** says that Job must be steeped in sin, and he calls Job to repent and be at peace with God. [23]**Job** maintains his innocence, and desires to argue with God face to face.

[24]Job questions why the wicked don't seem to experience judgement, and why in the end, both the wicked and the blameless seem to end up in the same place: the grave. [25]**Bildad** says that Job must be sinful. [26]**Job** rejects his friends' answers. He acknowledges the vastness of God's sovereignty and power, and questions whether anyone can truly understand the reason behind God's works. [27]He retains his innocence, and trusts that God's justice is perfect. [28]He asks the question: where can wisdom be found? He concludes that the fear of the Lord is wisdom, and to turn away from evil is understanding. [29]He longingly considers his

past; how he has walked in righteousness throughout his life, helping the needy and honouring God. [30]He considers how everyone, including God, seems to be against him. [31]He retains his innocence, describing his righteous deeds that he's carried out since childhood. However, he provides a conditional statement: that if he has indeed fallen into sin, he accepts the punishment fitting that sin.

[32]A younger man, **Elihu**, introduces himself and prepares to rebuke Job and his friends. [33]He rebukes Job, saying that God's wisdom is higher than any man's, and that Job is sinful. [34]He speaks about God's justice and Job's wickedness. [35]He says that God is not responding to Job because Job is prideful and without knowledge. [36]He extols God for his power and righteousness, and [37]calls Job to stop and consider God's wondrous works, for God will not regard the proud.

[38-39]**God** asks Job whether he knows how creation is governed. [40]God questions whether a faultfinder should contend with Him, and Job humbly stops speaking. [41]God continues to speak of His sovereignty in contrast to man's powerlessness. [42]**Job** humbly repents, acknowledging the superior wisdom of God. **God** rebukes Job's friends, and tells them to offer sacrifices for forgiveness. God restores Job to his former wealth, and more. Job dies; an old man, full of days.

Psalms

[1]The blessed man delights in God's word, while the wicked do not. [2]The blessed man takes refuge in God's Son. [3]God is our shield and defender; salvation belongs to Him. [4]God is to be trusted. He answers His peoples' prayers, [5]leads His people in righteousness, [6]hears His people's cries for help, and [7]judges righteously. [8]He is majestic and sovereign, yet He still cares for people. [9]Give thanks to God! Recount His wonderful deeds!

[10]God's wrath is not always immediate; the wicked sometimes prosper before they die. [11]God is righteous and He loves righteous deeds; the righteous shall see His face. [12]He protects the needy from the wicked. [13]His answers to prayer are not always immediate, but He is trustworthy.

[14]No one is righteous and Israel needs salvation. [15]Those who act righteously will dwell with God, and [16]in God's presence there is fullness of joy. [17]God is our protector and [18]powerful refuge. He equips His people to do what is right. [19]His word is perfect; it sanctifies His people. [20]Trust in the name of the Lord our God!

[21]The king trusts in God and remains strong because of God's love. [22]God's answers to prayer are not always immediate, but He is holy and mighty to save. [23]He is a good shepherd and shows His people mercy. [24]He is the strong, mighty King of glory, and [25]His friendship is for those who keep His covenant. We need God to forgive us.

[26]The psalmist loves God and wants Him to be gracious towards him. [27]God is light and salvation, so we shouldn't fear man. [28]God is the strength and saving refuge of His people, so trust in Him. [29]He is sovereign and powerful. [30]In His favour is life, and in His momentary anger is justice. [31]He is loving, so commit your spirit into His hands. [32]Blessed are those who are forgiven by God, so confess your sins and trust in Him for forgiveness. [33]God is upright, faithful, just and loving, so trust in His holy name! [34]Taste and see that the Lord is good! Take refuge in Him!

[35]God delights in the welfare of His people. [36]His steadfast love is a precious thing. [37]He upholds the righteous, but the wicked will perish. [38]We need God's help, for we are sinful and weak, but He is salvation. [39]Life is short but God is great, so hope in Him. [40]God helps His people, so rejoice in Him. [41]We need God's grace. [42]Even when times are tough, trust in God. [43]Even when enemies are provoking you, trust in God. [44]God's people do suffer. Any victory won by God's people is ultimately accomplished by God. [45]He is an eternal, righteous king. [46]He is our fortress and our refuge. [47]He is king over all the Earth. Praise Him!

[48]Zion – God's city – is awesome. God is powerful and loving. [49]Don't be fearful in times of trouble. Don't trust in wealth, which is fleeting, but trust in the eternal God. [50]He is a powerful judge. We are to be thankful to Him, and we should follow Him. [51]David wants God to forgive him and cleanse him of his sin. He wants God to sanctify him, so that he can live for God in all his ways. [52]Those who reject God and trust in their riches will be destroyed.

[53]There is no one who does good; no one who understands. God must save His people. [54]God is our Helper; He upholds our lives. [55]Cast all your burdens on God in prayer, for He won't permit the righteous to be moved. [56]Put your trust in God. If He is for us, we have no reason to fear those who are against us. [57]God is merciful and powerful. Even when danger surrounds us, we should still trust in God, and pray: Be exalted, O God, above the heavens! Let your glory be over all the Earth!

[58]God will judge the Earth. He will bring destruction for the wicked, but reward for His people. [59]The psalmist prays that God would deliver him from his enemies. Praise God, for He is our refuge. [60]The psalmist prays that God would help him against his foes. God brings about salvation and victory for His people. [61]The psalmist delights in God and yearns for His presence. [62]Trust in God at all times, for He is our rock and refuge. [63]The psalmist delights in God; His love is better than life; He is eternally satisfying.

[64]God ultimately foils the plans of the wicked in death. [65]God is sovereign over all the Earth, and salvation belongs to Him. [66]He is sovereign in protecting Israel and He is worthy of all praise. [67]He is a sovereign saviour who is worthy of praise. He is a fair judge, so we should be glad! [68]God saves and looks after His people, but He condemns and destroys those who reject Him. [69]The psalmist prays that God would show mercy to him, and that God would justly punish his enemies. [70]The psalmist asks God to deliver him from oppression without delay. [71]God is our refuge, and we should tell of his salvation and mighty deeds to everyone.

[72]The king prays that God would show him justice and kindness, and that God would be a blessing towards the people of Israel. [73]Even though it

seems like the wicked prosper, it is the wicked who will perish and the faithful who will be with God eternally. [74]The psalmist prays that God would uphold the covenant He has established with His people. [75]God is a just judge; He brings down the wicked and lifts up the righteous. [76]God is powerful and His judgement is coming. [77]He is powerful and eternally faithful. [78]We are to tell coming generations of the goodness, justice, wrath, and love of God.

[79]Jerusalem lies in ruins. The psalmist asks God how long His anger will last, and he prays for mercy. [80]The psalmist pleads that God would restore Israel and let His face shine upon them. [81]Israel didn't listen to God, and therefore God gave them over to their stubborn hearts. [82]God is judge over all the Earth. He rescues the weak and the needy. [83]The psalmist wants God to judge the nations and let the wicked perish. [84]The psalmist longs for the courts of God. Blessed are those who desire God and His presence. [85]The psalmist prays that God would continue to forgive and revive Israel. [86]God abounds in love for all who call upon Him. [87]God's city – Zion – is a glorious city. [88]The anguished psalmist cries out to God day and night in prayer. [89]The psalmist rejoices in the love of God, His holiness, and His promises to David, and he pleads to God to remember His promises and stay faithful to Israel. [90]The psalmist acknowledges God's eternality and his own life's brevity, and he asks for grace. [91]God delivers, protects, answers, rescues, satisfies, and saves His people. [92]Give thanks to God for His mighty works; in saving and preserving His people.

[93]God is holy, powerful and sovereign. [94]God is a refuge for His people, but He powerfully condemns the wicked. [95]Praise God, for He is a great King. [96]Sing to the Lord. Declare His glory among the nations. Ascribe

glory to God and worship Him in the splendour of His holiness. [97]The Lord reigns! Those who trust in Him have reason to rejoice! [98]God has made his righteousness and His salvation known to the nations. Sing to God and rejoice in Him! [99]God is holy! Praise His awesome name! [100]God is good: His steadfast love endures forever. Know this, and live for God! [101]The psalmist promises to love/do good, and hate/abstain from evil. [102]The psalmist considers his weakness and brevity in contrast to God's power and eternality. [103]Bless the Lord! God's steadfast love abounds to all His people! [104]God is sovereign over all the Earth: he cares for it and sustains it. Praise God!

[105]The psalmist recounts the works that God performed in saving Israel. Remembering God's works should lead us to praise God and tell others of His mighty works. [106]The psalmist recounts the rebellious acts of Israel, and how God remained faithful in preserving Israel despite their sinfulness. [107]God is sovereign in redeeming people; bringing them from spiritual death to spiritual life. [108]God is sovereign in helping Israel overcome its enemies. [109]The needy psalmist asks God to protect him and defeat his accusers.

[110]The psalmist speaks of a mighty sceptre being sent out of Zion; an eternal priest who will save His people and execute judgement on the nations. [111]God's awesome power is demonstrated in His works; especially in His saving of Israel. [112]Blessed is the one who fears God and delights in His commandments. [113]God is gloriously holy; we should praise Him! [114]God is sovereign and holy; we should fear Him. [115]The psalmist prays that God's name would be glorified, because God is greater than the idols of man. We ought to fear and trust God, because He is good and He blesses His people.

[116]The psalmist loves God because God hears his prayer and answers it. [117]God's faithfulness endures forever. Therefore, He is worthy of praise. [118]God's people ought to acknowledge the enduring nature of God's love, and respond in praise and prayer. The psalmist prays that God would open to him the gates of righteousness. [119]The psalmist delights in God's word and keeps God's commandments. He prays against his enemies who don't obey God, and he prays that God would give him salvation. [120]He prays that God would deliver him from his enemies who make war with their words. [121]God helps His people and keeps them from evil. [122]The psalmist prays for peace for Jerusalem. [123]He looks to God for mercy [124]and considers what Israel would be like without God's help. [125]Those who trust in God are safe; God surrounds his people and protects them. [126]The psalmist prays that God would restore the fortunes of Israel.

[127]Work is done in vain when it is not done by God's strength. Children are a blessing from God. [128]Those who fear God are blessed. [129]The psalmist prays that those who are against Israel would be put to shame. [130]Wait for God in prayer; hope in God always! He is our love and our salvation. [131]The psalmist humbly calms and quiets his soul as he hopes in God. [132]The psalmist recounts God's promise to David – the Davidic covenant from 2 Samuel 7. [133]It is so good and pleasant when brothers dwell in unity. [134]Bless the Lord. [135]The psalmist talks about God bringing Israel out of Egypt, and calls Israel to praise God. [136]Give thanks to God, for his steadfast love endures forever!

[137]The psalmist is in Babylon and he doesn't want to forget his home land – Jerusalem. He longs for it. [138]The psalmist thanks God for exalting His

name and word above all things. The psalmist trusts God with his whole life. [139]God searches us and knows us. He is all-knowing. The psalmist asks God to slay the wicked and to search him, to see if any wickedness is in him, and to lead him in the way everlasting. [140]God protects the needy and carries out just judgement on the wicked. [141]The psalmist prays that God would keep him from joining in the sinful practices of the wicked. [142]God is a refuge for us when people persecute us. [143]The psalmist's soul thirsts for God, and prays that God would deliver him from his enemies. [144]God's people are blessed, because God is their fortress; able to rescue them from strife. [145]God is great: His works are great; He is gracious; He hears and answers prayer. [146]Blessed is he whose help is God. [147]Praise the Lord! He exalts the humble; protects His people; sustains all things. [148]All creation ought to praise God, for He created everything and rules over everything. [149]God's people ought to praise God, for He saved them and allows them to execute judgement. [150]Praise God!

Proverbs

[1]The fear of the Lord is the beginning of knowledge, but fools despise wisdom and discipline. Consider cautiously who you follow and imitate. Repent, and God will make his word known to you by his Spirit. Whoever listens to God will dwell secure and be at ease. [2]Wisdom comes from God and His word. Seek wisdom, and you will keep to the paths of the righteous, and you will be delivered from sinful ways. [3]Trust God with all your heart; don't lean on your own understanding; God will make straight your paths. Wisdom is more valuable than wealth. [4]Consider how you live your life. Listen to God's word and follow the righteous path; don't trust in yourself and don't take the wicked path. [5]All sin, including sexual sin, leads to death. Be above reproach; flee temptations to sin sexually.

[6]The author gives practical warnings. He describes the worthless man; He outlines what God hates; He warns against adultery. [7]The author uses the story of an adulteress to warn against sexual sin. The temptations are everywhere, and they are deceitful and compelling, but we must remember that sin leads to death, not joy. [8]Wisdom is more precious than wealth. Wisdom comes from our eternal God. Whoever finds wisdom finds life. [9]Wisdom and folly are both personified as women who call out in their towns. Wisdom involves fearing God and knowing Him; wisdom leads to life. Folly involves sin and deceit; folly leads to death. [10]The righteous man gains wisdom; he is blessed indeed. The wicked man dwells in folly; he is heading for destruction. [11]The righteous man will flourish and will be delivered from death; the wicked will perish.

[12]The righteous man is diligent and upright; the wicked are self-centred, and are lead to death. [13]The righteous man heeds instruction, and is rewarded and satisfied; the wicked perish unsatisfied. [14]The righteous man fears God and discerns his own steps; the wicked run to sin and destruction. [15]The righteous man seeks knowledge and reproof in a gentle spirit. He prays fervently and pursues righteousness; the wicked stubbornly walk in the path of folly.

[16]God is sovereign and just. Blessed is he who trusts in the Lord! Blessed is he who walks in humility and truthfulness. [17]The righteous man seeks wisdom and peace, and flees from folly; the wicked set their minds on Earthly things, and are steeped in sin. [18]The righteous man runs to God as his strength and refuge, and seeks knowledge diligently; the wicked are ruined by the words they speak in foolishness. [19]The righteous man is generous and rests satisfied in the fear of the Lord; the wicked are lazy and heading for condemnation. [20]The righteous man stays away from strife and evil. He is diligent, faithful, and seeks understanding. [21]Whoever pursues righteousness and kindness will find life, righteousness and honour. The wicked will perish.

[22]Guard your soul: love purity of heart and gracious speech, and trust in God. [23]Do not set your heart on Earthly things – money, sex, and alcohol. Continue in the fear of the Lord; apply your heart to instruction; be holy. [24]Do not envy the wicked, but rescue them by telling them about God's goodness. [25]Strive for humility, gracious speech, and wisdom to deal with your neighbours and enemies. [26]People who are proud, foolish, sluggish, or quarrelsome are without wisdom and honour. Act with wisdom towards these people. [27]Be humble, and be a good friend. Be a faithful

brother in Christ. Keep your heart from sin. [28]Seek the Lord and uphold justice for all.

[29]The righteous man will abound with blessings; the wicked will not go unpunished. [30]The word of God is true and powerful. Use your tongue and time in a God-exalting way. Repent of all your pride and foolishness. [31]Defend the rights of the poor and needy. Wives are to fear the Lord, maintaining a diligent, holy lifestyle.

Ecclesiastes

[1]The preacher explains that all is vanity. You can't be satisfied in the world and what it offers. There's nothing new under the sun. Seeking wisdom and seeking folly are both strivings after wind.

[2]The preacher spent time seeking pleasure and indulgence, but this was vanity. He spent time seeking after wisdom, and he realised that there is more gain in wisdom than folly, even though both paths lead to the same end. He sees that toil and labour is also vanity. He sees that the best one can hope for is to find enjoyment in his toil and in God's gifts of food and drink. [3]The preacher acknowledges that there is a time for everything; for mourning and laughing, for speaking and silence, and so on. The preacher again realises that there is nothing better for man to do than to rejoice in his work. He sees that both man and beast live and die the same, for all is vanity. [4]The preacher considers all the oppression that happens in the world. He continues to see that labour is done in vain, but he notes that two or three people working together is better than one. He notes again that wisdom is greater than folly.

[5]The preacher says to be cautious in prayer; to let your words be few, and to fear God. He says that a lover of money will not be satisfied. He maintains that it is good to find enjoyment in one's toil: this power to enjoy is a gift from God. [6]The preacher says that it is an evil when man cannot find joy or satisfaction in his toil; when God does not give him the power to do so. [7]The preacher contrasts wisdom and folly. The house of mourning is better than the house of feasting; a wise man's rebuke is

better than a fool's song; patience is better than pride. The preacher sees God's sovereignty as a comfort. He notes something which is worse than death: a treacherous woman. He considers the depravity of man. [8]The preacher says it's good to keep the king's command, and to fear God. He acknowledges that the wicked don't always seem to get what they deserve on Earth. He reaffirms the goodness of finding joy in one's work. [9]The preacher contemplates this evil; that everyone – the wise and the foolish – eventually dies. He says that those headed for Sheol should eat bread, drink wine, and be glad while they can. He continues to contemplate wisdom as more valuable than folly or military strength. [10]The preacher continues to prize wisdom above folly. He sees another evil in the world; that people in positions of high authority often aren't suited or qualified for the job, and that those in low places would often to a better job.

[11]The preacher calls for people to acknowledge their lack of knowledge; to acknowledge that anything can happen at any time on Earth. He tells youth to enjoy themselves but to remember that judgement is coming. [12]The preacher tells youth to remember their creator before they get old and find no pleasure in life; before they grow old and die. The preacher ends by exhorting people to fear God and keep his commandments, because God is going to judge everyone in the end.

The Song of Solomon

[1]The woman loves the king and wants to be with him. She says that while she is not beautiful, she still wants to be with the king. The king calls her beautiful, and she calls him beautiful. Their friends approve. [2]The woman again says that she is not beautiful – a simple rose of Sharon. But the man says she is beautiful – a rose among brambles. The woman delights in the king's physical embrace, and in his voice, which calls her to come away with him.

[3]The woman can't find the king, so she rises from her bed and wanders the city in search for him. She finds him and brings him home. The king makes for himself a carriage and goes to the woman to get married, and they celebrate. [4]The king admires the woman's beauty – her hair, teeth, lips, cheeks, neck and breasts. He is totally captivated by her. [5]The two come together and enjoy each other. Later, the woman again can't find the king. She goes out to search for him, but she is beaten up by city watchmen. She goes to her friends for help to find the king, and the friends ask why she desires the king so much. The woman explains her admiration; she admires his head, hair, eyes, cheeks, lips, arms, legs; the king is her beloved and her friend. [6]The two find each other again and the king describes her beauty to her; her eyes, hair, teeth and cheeks. [7]The king continues to describe her beauty, and she tells him to come with her into the fields to share their love.

[8]Friends ask for advice for a sister who is not physically attractive, and the woman gives her advice. The king and the woman continue to yearn for one another and give themselves for one another.

OLD TESTAMENT

PROPHETS

Isaiah

[1]Isaiah receives a vision concerning Judah and Jerusalem. Judah is horrifically sinful, but God promises future redemption for the repentant. [2]All nations shall come to know God. God promises to utterly destroy the idols of the world. God alone will be exalted as sovereign in the end. [3]God will judge Judah and Jerusalem for their sin.

[4]God speaks of a day when the "Branch of the Lord" will be glorious, and the sin of Israel will be dealt with, and there will be redemption – restoration and rest for God's people.

[5]God compares Israel to a vineyard that has produced the wrong type of fruit. He promises to destroy and remove the wicked from Israel. God's people will go into exile and be humbled, and He will be exalted in justice. He will use other nations to carry out punishment on Israel.

[6]Isaiah sees a glorious vision of the Lord. God calls Isaiah to be a prophet to His people, but says that Isaiah's ministry will have a hardening effect on his generation. [7]The Northern Kingdom will be shattered. Isaiah prophesies foreign invasion. God will give a sign: a son called Immanuel, born of a virgin. This sign will give God's people hope that God is truly with them.

[8]The king of Assyria will attack Damascus, Samaria and Judah. [9]God will be a sanctuary to all who keep His testimony and fear Him, but there will be gloom and anguish for those who don't. [10]Assyria will take Israel into

exile. However, God's wrath will be poured out on Assyria as well, and a remnant of the people of Israel and Judah will return to Jerusalem.

[11]There shall come forth a descendent of Jesse who will be righteous and faithful. There will come a day when enemies – wolf and lamb – will dwell together in harmony. The Earth will be full of the knowledge of God, and God will save His people from all over the Earth. [12]On that day, people will rejoice. For while God was angry at His people, His anger turned away, that He might comfort them and be their salvation.

[13]God will overthrow and destroy Babylon. [14]God will save a remnant of Israel, but He will destroy Babylon, Assyria, Philistia, [15-16]Moab, [17]Damascus, [18]and Cush. [19]He will make Egypt desolate, but some will turn to God and receive mercy and healing. [20]The king of Assyria shall capture Egypt and Cush. [21]Babylon will fall, and Kedar will come to an end. [22]Despite various defensive attempts, Jerusalem will be broken. A steward named Shebna will be replaced by another called Eliakim, but he too will fall. [23]Tyre will be destroyed. [24]The Earth is defiled because mankind has transgressed God's laws. Judgement is coming.

[25]God will swallow up death forever. Tears will be wiped away and reproach will be removed. We should rejoice in the salvation that God gives. [26]We should earnestly trust God and rejoice in His sovereignty. His judgement is coming, but so is resurrection. [27]God protects His people by punishing their enemies. Israel shall blossom and fill the whole Earth with fruit. Israel's guilt will be atoned for. [28]Ephraim will be trodden underfoot. Jerusalem will be purged of its lies. Although God's people have made a covenant with death, God will lay a precious cornerstone – a sure foundation – which is salvation for all who believe. [29]God will

judge Israel and its enemies, and shall bring them low. However, because God's true people draw near with their lips – even though their hearts are distant – God will again do wonderful things for them. The deaf shall hear, the blind shall see, and the meek shall obtain fresh joy in God.

[30]Israel's trust in Egypt and other foreign nations for protection is a big mistake. Israel doesn't listen to God's word or the prophets. However, in returning to God and trusting in Him, Israel shall be saved, for God waits upon His people to be gracious to them. [31]Israel's trust in Egypt will lead to failure. Israel must turn back to God and trust Him.

[32]A king will come and reign in righteousness. Complacent women should tremble, because the harvest will fail and the city will be deserted. However, the Spirit will be poured out on God's people, so that righteousness will abide in them, bringing about peace and trust. [33]God's kingdom will be filled with justice and righteousness. Only the righteous will be able to dwell with God, who is our judge, law-giver, and king. Sinners will be cast out, as will sickness and iniquity. [34]God is enraged against the nations, and he has devoted them to destruction, but [35]God will ransom and save his people. The blind, deaf, lame and mute shall be healed. God's people shall experience everlasting joy as they walk in the way of holiness.

[36]During Hezekiah's reign in Judah, the king of Assyria comes to Judah and taunts the people. He tells them not to trust in God or listen to Hezekiah, but to obey him. The Israelites refuse, and remain faithful to God and return back to Hezekiah. [37]A prophet called Isaiah tells Hezekiah to continue to trust in God. Isaiah says that God will protect Judah against Assyria. Hezekiah prays for salvation, and God strikes down many

Assyrians, and the king departs and goes home to Assyria. Later, the king of Assyria is killed by his sons. [38]Hezekiah falls ill. He prays that God would heal him, and God does so. [39]Hezekiah welcomes the king of Babylon into his house, and Isaiah predicts that Babylon will take Israel into exile.

[40]One will come to prepare the way for the Lord in the wilderness, and the glory of God shall be revealed. Our everlasting, sovereign God is coming with reward and recompense. This is good news! [41]God will judge the nations. Israel shouldn't fear, for God is with them and he will uphold them. [42]God will send a Spirit-filled servant who will bring forth justice to the nations. We should rejoice in our salvation. [43]God loves Israel. He will gather His people from all nations and save them by blotting out their transgressions, for their salvation and for His glory. [44]God will pour out His Spirit on Israel and their offspring. There is only one God: our redeemer and Lord. He hates idolatry, but He loves and redeems Israel.

[45]God will use Cyrus in such a way as to show all people that there is only one God. Idolatrous foreign nations will be put to shame, but God's people will be saved and kept for all eternity. [46]There is only one God and He created and sustains all things, so idolatry is foolish. [47]God will destroy Babylon because it puts its faith in pleasure and sorcery.

[48]God speaks a new thing to Israel: He will defer His anger from Israel and redeem Israel for the sake of His glory. [49]God will be glorified through His servant, who will be a light for the nations, so that salvation may reach to the ends of the Earth. [50]God's servant is perfect. He sustains the weary, refuses temptations to sin, and accepts persecution. We should trust in God and enjoy peaceful reliance on Him. [51]God is

Israel's comforter. He will set forth His justice as a light to the peoples. His righteousness draws near and His salvation goes out. Those who trust in God shall obtain everlasting joy. [52]Israel will be redeemed and all the Earth shall see the salvation God gives. God's servant will be exalted despite his marred physical appearance. [53]God's servant will be despised and rejected. He will be smitten by God and wounded for our transgressions. By his death we shall be healed, because God will lay on him our iniquities. He will be silent unto death. He will die alongside the wicked. He will be buried in a rich setting. He will again see life and will make many to be accounted righteous. [54]God will show compassion to His people with everlasting love. [55]Those that thirst should come to the Lord. True satisfaction is found in Him alone. [56]God will save foreigners who put their trust in Him. Selfish leaders have no place in God's kingdom. [57]There is no peace for those who are stubbornly idolatrous. But God will rescue those of contrite and lowly spirit.

[58]When Israel fast, they seek their own pleasure and they suppress the poor. This fasting is not acceptable to God. However, when Israel keep the Sabbath and care for the poor and love their neighbours, then God will accept their fasting. [59]Israel's sin separates them from God. God will judge the nations, and a redeemer will come to save those in Israel who repent. [60]There will come a time when God's people rest in God's kingdom. Everyone will be righteous and peace will abound. [61]God's servant will bring good news of liberty and salvation to God's people. [62]Israel's salvation is coming. They shall no longer be forsaken, because God shall rejoice over them. [63]God will be victorious over evil and He will care for His people as He has always done. [64]Israel have all become unclean through sin, but God won't remember their iniquity forever. [65]God's servants will be saved and given a new earth to enjoy for

eternity, but those who forsake God will be destroyed. [66]God will save the humble and contrite in spirit. But He will judge and destroy those who rebel against Him.

Jeremiah

[1]God tells Jeremiah that he will be a prophet to the nations. God will judge the northern tribes for forsaking Him. [2]God called Israel to be holy, but they've gone their own way and forgotten Him. [3]God calls faithless Israel and treacherous Judah to return to Him and acknowledge their guilt. If they return, God will show them mercy. [4]God will bring disaster upon Judah because of their wickedness. [5]God will use a foreign nation to strike Israel and Judah, but a remnant will be kept alive within a foreign country. [6]God will bring disaster upon Jerusalem because of their refusal to pay attention to God.

[7]God tells Jeremiah to stand at the gate of the Temple and urge everyone to repent. If they do, God will let them dwell in the land peacefully. But if they don't, God will cast them out of His sight. [8]God will bring doom upon Israel because of their perpetual backsliding. [9]Jeremiah weeps because of Israel's wickedness and impending destruction. God will scatter them among the nations and will punish those who are circumcised merely in the flesh. [10]God is an everlasting king, while idols are worthless objects awaiting destruction, so Israel ought to follow God. [11]God will bring disaster on Judah because they've broken the covenant that He made to Abraham.

[12]Jeremiah complains to God and asks Him why the wicked prosper. God says that everyone is wicked, and that He is still just. He will pluck up everyone from the land and will bring each to their heritage. He will allow anyone to be a part of His people if they obey Him. [13]God uses a

spoiled linen cloth to illustrate how he will spoil Judah's pride. He uses jars of wine to illustrate how he will fill the inhabitants of the land with drunkenness, so that they will destroy each other. Judah will be taken into exile because of their iniquity.

[14]Jeremiah wants God to relent from his anger. False prophets say that God will relent, but He won't; He will bring disaster upon Judah. [15]God will use sword, dogs, birds and beasts to destroy Judah, because of the sinfulness of King Manasseh. Jeremiah complains – he loves God and His word and yet he is given to destruction. So God promises to save and deliver Jeremiah if he returns to God from all wickedness. [16]God tells Jeremiah not to have a family, because men, women and children shall die of deadly diseases. He tells Jeremiah not to mourn for the people or feast with the people, because God has taken peace away from Israel and has silenced gladness. God will exile His people into foreign lands because of their sin, but He shall preserve and return a remnant of His people. [17]God will make Judah serve their enemies in foreign lands, because they've trusted in man and not in God. Jeremiah prays for his own deliverance. God tells Jeremiah to tell people to keep the Sabbath day holy.

[18]God uses a potter and clay to illustrate his ability to shape disaster against Israel because of their wickedness. The people plot against Jeremiah and refuse to pay attention to him, and Jeremiah prays for disaster to come upon the people. [19]God uses a broken flask to illustrate how he will break Judah and Jerusalem. [20]A priest named Pashhur persecutes Jeremiah because he doesn't like what Jeremiah is prophesying. God says he will give Pashhur and his household into the hands of the king of Babylon, along with all of Judah. They will be exiled.

Jeremiah will continue to prophecy despite persecution, by God's strength.

[21]King Zedekiah (see 2 Kings 24) inquires of Jeremiah to see if God will prevent Nebuchadnezzar king of Babylon from attacking Judah. God says He Himself will strike Judah with pestilence, sword and famine, and will hand over the survivors to Nebuchadnezzar. [22]Kings who do justice and righteousness will receive peace, while those who disobey will receive desolation. King Jehoahaz, king Jehoiakim and king Jehoiachin (see 2 Kings 23-24) will die in foreign lands because of their wickedness.

[23]God will raise up a righteous Branch; a wise king who will execute justice and righteousness. In his days Judah and Israel will be saved. God will bring disaster upon false prophets and adulterous priests who speak lies and take His people astray.

[24]God uses a basket of good figs and a basket of bad figs to illustrate that He will regard the exiles who go to Babylon as good. He will love them, bring them back into Canaan, and give them hearts to know Him as their Lord. However, God will bring disaster upon Zedekiah, those who remain in the land of Canaan instead of going into exile, and those who dwell in Egypt.

[25]God will send Judah into captivity in Babylon for seventy years, and then he will punish the king of Babylon. God gives Jeremiah a cup of His wrath to give to many nations to drink. This drink will make the nations drunk, so that God can bring destruction upon these nations. [26]God tells Jeremiah to go to the Temple and to warn people that disobedience to God will result in the destruction of the Temple. The people at the

Temple threaten Jeremiah with death, but he is spared. [27]God uses a yoke-bar on Jeremiah's neck to illustrate how Israel and its surrounding nations shall be exiled to Babylon to serve Nebuchadnezzar. God tells Zedekiah king of Judah to take His people and go willingly to Babylon, because anyone who doesn't go will die. God tells him not to listen to false prophets who prophesy peace.

[28]A false prophet called Hananiah comes to the Temple and says that he will break the yoke of the king of Babylon. Jeremiah prophesies Hananiah's death, and he dies. [29]Jeremiah sends a letter to the exiles in Babylon, telling them to build houses and have families in the land, because they will be living there for seventy years. After that, God will bring them back to Canaan, and they will seek God and find Him. God will destroy those who didn't go into exile, and he will punish the false prophet Shemaiah who undermined Jeremiah's words. [30]God will restore the fortunes of His people; He will bring them out of Babylon and plant them again in Canaan, where they shall serve the Lord their God and David their king. God struck Israel because of their flagrant sinfulness, and He will heal them because of His love for them. [31]God will turn His peoples' mourning into joy as He brings them back to Canaan. He will make a new covenant with them: He will put His law within them and write it on their hearts. He will be their God and they will be His people. He will forgive their iniquity and remember their sin no more.

[32]While Nebuchadnezzar is besieging Jerusalem, Jeremiah is told by God to buy his cousin's field. Jeremiah prays for understanding, and God says that He will gather the exiles and bring them back to Canaan, where life will continue under a new, everlasting covenant. [33]God will restore the fortunes of Judah after exile. He will forgive all the guilt of their sin. He

will cause a righteous Branch to spring up for David, and Judah will be saved. [34]King Zedekiah will be taken into exile in Babylon, but he will experience a peaceful death and an honourable burial. God will punish those who disobeyed Zedekiah's command to set free the slaves in the land.

[35]Jeremiah takes a family called the Rechabites into a chamber and offers them wine. They refuse the wine because their father had told them never to drink wine. God contrasts their obedience with the disobedience of Judah. [36]God tells Jeremiah to write all the words that He has told him on a scroll, and Jeremiah does so. His scribe Baruch takes the scroll and speaks the words in the Temple, then in the king's house, then to King Jehoiakim, who burns the scroll. God tells Jeremiah to rewrite the scroll, including judgements on Jehoiakim, who will die because of his stubbornness.

[37]King Zedekiah asks Jeremiah to pray for Judah. Jeremiah does so, and God tells him that Judah will be captured by the Babylonians. Jeremiah travels towards the land of Benjamin but is mistakenly put in prison when someone thinks he's going to join the Babylonians. Jeremiah tells Zedekiah what God told him, and Zedekiah lets him out of prison. [38]Jeremiah is put into a well because of his prophecies. A man from the king's house rescues him, and he goes to Zedekiah and warns him again that if he surrenders, he will live, but if he doesn't, he will die.

[39]The Babylonian army captures Jerusalem. The poorest Israelites are allowed to stay in Judah. Nebuchadnezzar allows Jeremiah to stay in Judah with a trusted Israelite called Gedaliah. Everyone else, including King Zedekiah, is taken to Babylon. [40]Nebuchadnezzar appoints Gedaliah

governor in Judah during the exile. Jeremiah stays and lives with him among the people in Judah. Judean army captains who had run away during the siege return to Judah when they hear that Gedaliah is governor there. They warn Gedaliah that the king of the Ammonites is sending a man called Ishmael to kill him, but Gedaliah doesn't believe it. [41]The Ammonite king sends an official called Ishmael who comes and kills Gedaliah as well as some Judeans who were with him. Ishmael takes the rest of the Judeans hostage and sets out to go back to Ammon. However the Judean army captains chase after him and confront him in Gideon. Ishmael flees alone. All the Judeans go and stay near Bethlehem, intending to go to Egypt to avoid Babylonian soldiers. [42]God tells Jeremiah and the remnant of Israelites to stay in Judah. If they stay in Judah, God will build them up and protect them against king Nebuchadnezzar. But if they flee to Egypt, God will destroy them.

[43]The people accuse Jeremiah of lying. The army captains take everyone, including Jeremiah, down to Egypt to live there. In Egypt, God says to them that Nebuchadnezzar will come and strike Egypt. [44]God says He will destroy the remnant of Judah that has gone to Egypt. The remnant tells Jeremiah to make offerings to a false god, and Jeremiah refuses and rebukes them. God will strike them, but a few of them shall survive and return to Judah. [45]God tells Jeremiah's scribe, Baruch, that He will bring disaster upon all flesh, but Baruch's life shall be spared. [46]Nebuchadnezzar will strike the land of Egypt and take its inhabitants into exile. [47]God will destroy Philistia, [48]Moab, [49]Ammon, Edom, Damascus, Kedar, Hazor and Elam. [50]God will bring disaster upon Babylon from the North, but Israel and Judah shall join together in an everlasting covenant with God. [51]God will send the Medes to bring utter destruction upon Babylon because of their wickedness.

[52]Nebuchadnezzar comes with his army against Jerusalem and destroys it. They destroy the Temple, the king's palace and the walls in Jerusalem. They capture Zedekiah and others and take them into exile, but they leave the poorest Judeans in the land. Eventually, Evil-merodach becomes king of Babylon, and he graciously frees Jehoiachin – a former king in Judah – and treats him well for the rest of his life.

Lamentations

[1]The author describes Jerusalem – a city which was once full of people but now lies in ruins. God has made the people of Judah dwell in distress among the nations because of their sinfulness. [2]The people of Judah sit on the ground in anguish and their enemies rejoice.

[3]The author is a man who has seen affliction under the rod of God's wrath. His enemies taunt him and he is in anguish, but he has hope in God because He is sovereign over everything and His mercies never come to an end.

[4]Jerusalem lies in ruins and its people stoop in anguish. No one believed that Jerusalem could be captured, but it was, because of its sinfulness. The people trusted in Zedekiah, but he was taken captive. Jerusalem's punishment is accomplished, but Edom's is yet to come. [5]Everyone from Jerusalem is suffering because of the disaster that has come upon them. Jerusalem has fallen because of its sinfulness, but God reigns forever and His throne endures to all generations. The author pleads to God for restoration and renewal.

Ezekiel

[1]The word of the Lord comes to Ezekiel the priest while he is in Babylon. He sees a stormy wind from which come four living creatures, all with strange appearances. They follow the spirit in whatever it does. Ezekiel hears a voice and sees a majestic throne, upon which sits a likeness of a human appearance. [2]The one on the throne speaks to Ezekiel. He is sending Ezekiel to the people of Israel, who have rebelled against him. He tells Ezekiel not to be afraid, and gives him a scroll with words of lamentation written on it. [3]God tells Ezekiel to eat the scroll and to go and speak to the exiles, and Ezekiel does so. God says that Ezekiel will be a watchman over the house of Israel who will give them warnings. Ezekiel will be mute, and will only be able to speak when God gives him a message to speak.

[4]God tells Ezekiel to build a small siege works around a single brick, to act as a sign for the house of Israel. Ezekiel lies down next to the siege to illustrate the time that Israel and Judah will spend in punishment. [5]God tells Ezekiel to cut off his hair, and destroy the hair by fire, sword and scattering to the wind. God will execute judgements such as these against Jerusalem in the sight of the nations. [6]God will destroy the high places, idols, and idolaters within Israel. But God will let some people live, and they will remember Him among the nations. [7]God will bring destruction upon Israel because of its wickedness. [8]Ezekiel again sees a form that has the appearance of a man, and the man shows him a vision of all the abominable idols of Israel. [9]God sends executioners to kill all

the idolaters in Jerusalem, but He tells them not to harm anyone who has a special mark on them, signifying their abstinence from idolatry.

[10]God tells a man to get hot coals from the cherubim in the Temple, and to scatter them over Jerusalem. Ezekiel sees the glory of the Lord leaving the threshold of the Temple, along with the four living creatures with strange appearances. [11]God will bring punishment upon those who devise iniquity and give wicked council in Jerusalem. God tells Ezekiel that He will save a remnant of Israel; He will bring them out of exile and place them again in Canaan. He will give them a new heart and a new spirit to follow Him.

[12]Ezekiel goes to the first exiles in Babylon and makes for himself baggage like that of an exile. He brings out the baggage by day, as a sign to the exiles that others from Israel will be taken into captivity. [13]God tells him to prophesy against the false prophets of Israel, who pretend to speak God's words and predict peace when there is no peace. [14]God calls Israel to repent of idolatry. He will punish those who refuse to repent and He will bring disaster upon Jerusalem, but a righteous remnant will remain. [15]God will bring destruction upon Jerusalem, just as fire consumes a useless vine. [16]Israel is like an unfaithful bride – it trusted in the nations instead of trusting in God. Therefore God will bring disaster upon Israel, but one day He will atone for their sin and enter into a new covenant with them. [17]Ezekiel speaks a riddle to the house of Israel, involving two eagles (Babylon and Egypt) and a vine (Israel). The riddle illustrates that while being exiled, rather than humbling themselves before the Babylonians and keeping a covenant of peace with them, Israel tried to call to Egypt for help. Israel will suffer because of this action. [18]People will be held accountable for their sins, not the sins of

their fathers or sons. The righteous shall live; the wicked shall die. God does not take pleasure in the death of anyone, so He calls all to repent and live.

[19]Ezekiel laments for the princes of Israel. He speaks two metaphors: one about a lioness mother with two cubs who are taken to Babylon, and another about a vine with a weak stem, to illustrate the plight of the princes of Israel.

[20]Ezekiel speaks to the elders of Israel and recounts how God brought Israel out of Egypt and preserves them despite their wickedness. He has acted for the sake of His name, that it should not be profaned by the nations. But now God will scatter Israel in foreign countries, but a remnant will be saved and returned to Israel, where they will worship God sincerely.

[21]God will draw His sword against all flesh. [22]Israel has shed much blood and set up many idols, so God will strike them and and scatter them among the nations. [23]Samaria whored after Assyria, and God gave Samaria into their hands for destruction. Jerusalem whores after Babylon, and God will likewise give Jerusalem into their hands for destruction.

[24]The king of Babylon lays siege to Jerusalem, and Ezekiel compares Jerusalem to a boiling pot. Ezekiel's wife dies, but God tells him not to mourn or weep, because when God destroys Jerusalem its people will not mourn but shall simply groan to one another as they rot away in their sin. [25]God will execute vengeance on Ammon, Moab, Seir, Edom and Philistia, because of their wicked ways. [26]God will bring Tyre to a

dreadful end because they acted wickedly against Israel. God will send the king of Babylon to destroy them. [27]Ezekiel laments for Tyre, because it is a wealthy city with many trading partners. But God will bring Tyre to a dreadful end. [28]The Prince of Tyre has grown proud in his wealth, so God will bring him to an end. Ezekiel laments for the Prince of Tyre. God will also destroy Sidon. God will gather Israel from the nations, and they shall dwell securely in their own land. [29]God will make Egypt desolate because of their pride and deceptiveness. He will give Egypt into the hands of Nebuchadnezzar king of Babylon. [30]Ezekiel laments for Egypt, because God will use Nebuchadnezzar king of Babylon to put an end to the wealth of Egypt. [31]Pharaoh and his multitude shall be brought down and destroyed because of their pride. [32]Ezekiel laments for Egypt, because God will use Babylon to destroy them, and they shall descend to the grave along with the other destroyed nations. [33]God has set Ezekiel as a watchman over the house of Israel, to tell the people to repent. God has done this because he doesn't take pleasure in the death of the wicked, but He wants them to turn back and live. Jerusalem will become desolate because of its complacency and pride.

[34]Ezekiel prophesies against the self-seeking shepherds of Israel who refuse to nurture the sheep. God will rescue His sheep from among the nations and will provide for them. He will make a covenant of peace with them and will be their God, and He will set David as prince over them. [35]God will make Mount Seir desolate because it hated Israel, and [36]He will punish the nations surrounding Israel. He will bring His people back to the land of Canaan for the sake of His holy name being known among the nations, and He will give His people a new heart and spirit; they will be His people and He will be their God.

[37]Ezekiel enters a valley full of bones. God breathes life into the bones and they stand and live. God will put His Spirit within His people and He will put them in their own land. God tells Ezekiel to pick up two sticks and join them together, illustrating that God will join Israel and Judah together. His people will be one nation, David will be their king and prince, and God will save them from their sin. [38]When Israel are gathered back to their land and dwell securely, the land of Gog will come and attack Israel. On that day God's anger will be aroused; there shall be a great earthquake in the land and mountains will tumble down. Gog will be destroyed by sword, and God's greatness shall be known by many nations. [39]Gog will be defeated, and Israel will bury the people of Gog. They will celebrate with a feast prepared by God; they shall eat flesh and drink blood. God will set His glory among the nations, and they shall see His judgement. God will restore Israel and have mercy on them.

[40-42]During Babylonian exile, Ezekiel has a vision of a new temple in Israel. [43]He sees God's glory fill the temple, and God outlines the rules for the altar. [44]God's temple shall be holy. The Levites will minister in the temple, and God will be their inheritance. [45]God allots a portion of the land as a holy district for the temple and the Levites. He allots land for the prince. He calls for justice in the land, along with proper offerings and the Passover. [46]God gives rules concerning princes, priests, sacrifices and feasts. [47]Ezekiel sees water flowing out from underneath the temple towards the Arabah Sea. This water is a river, alongside which trees will grow to provide the people with food. [48]God allots portions of the land to each tribe of Israel.

Daniel

[1]**Nebuchadnezzar king of Babylon besieges Jerusalem** during the reign of Jehoiakim king of Judah. He brings exiles to Babylon, and supplies a group of them with food and education within his palace. Among these are **Daniel, Shadrach, Meshach and Abednego**. They stay faithful to God; they abstain from the king's food and grow in wisdom. They are chosen to stand before Nebuchadnezzar as hired servants.

[2]Nebuchadnezzar has a dream, and he seeks out magicians to tell him the dream and interpret it. No magician can do it, but God reveals the dream to Daniel, who goes to Nebuchadnezzar and interprets the dream. Daniel, Shadrach, Meshach and Abednego are all promoted. [3]Nebuchadnezzar makes a **golden idol**, and he commands all people to worship it. Shadrach, Meshach and Abednego refuse, so they are thrown into a **fiery furnace**. They survive the fire and are joined by a fourth figure. Nebuchadnezzar brings the three out of the furnace, and promises to punish anyone who blasphemes against the God of Israel.

[4]Nebuchadnezzar has a dream involving an impressive tree being chopped down. Daniel interprets the dream, saying that Nebuchadnezzar will be driven away, and he will dwell in the fields like an animal until he understands that God is king. It happens, and Nebuchadnezzar praises God and is re-established in Babylon.

[5]Nebuchadnezzar's son **Belshazzar** becomes king in Babylon. He prepares a feast for his staff, and they drink wine and praise false gods. A human

hand appears and writes a **message on the palace wall**. Daniel interprets the message for Belshazzar, saying that Babylon will be divided and given to the Medes and Persians. That night, Belshazzar is killed and Darius, a Mede, takes the kingdom. [6]Belshazzar plans to promote Daniel, so the other staff plot against him. They convince Belshazzar to order all people to worship him alone. Daniel refuses and continues to worship the true God, and he is thrown into a **den of lions**. He survives, and Belshazzar has the other staff thrown in. Belshazzar makes a decree that everyone is to fear Daniel's God.

[7]Daniel sees a **vision** of four great beasts who are four kings. He sees the Ancient of Days sitting on a throne with myriad people surrounding Him. He sees the greatest beast/king killed, and the other three live for a while after. He sees one like a **son of man** approach the Ancient of Days, and He is given dominion and glory and an everlasting kingdom. [8]Daniel sees a vision of a Ram with two horns (Media and Persia). The ram is defeated by a goat with a great horn (Greece). The great horn falls, and in its place four other horns/kingdoms arise. One of the horns grows exceedingly large. Likewise, an evil king shall arise who shall destroy many and rise up against the Prince of princes, but he shall be broken.

[9]Daniel prays to God and confesses the sin of Israel, and pleads for mercy upon Jerusalem. A man called Gabriel reveals to Daniel that there shall be seventy weeks in which to finish transgression, put an end to sin, atone for iniquity, bring in everlasting righteousness, and anoint a most holy place. An anointed prince shall come and establish a strong covenant with his people. [10]Daniel receives a vision of a majestic man in linen, who tells him that he has come to make him understand what is to happen to God's people in the latter days. The man has been opposed by

the prince of Persia, and he will fight against Persia with the help of a prince named Michael. When he does so, Greece will come. [11]The man in linen prophesies the oncoming **political tensions and military attacks** between areas and nations of the Near East, such as Persia, Greece, Egypt, the northern kingdoms and the southern kingdoms. [12]The man in linen says that there will come a time when Michael – the prince of God's people – shall arise. There shall be a time of trouble, but God's people will be delivered. **Those who sleep in the dust of the Earth shall awake: some to everlasting life, and some to everlasting contempt.**

Hosea

[1]**God tells Hosea to marry a whore**, because Israel has whored after other nations. Hosea marries a whore called Gomer. They bear two sons – Jezreel and Not My People – and a daughter named No Mercy. God will punish the house of Jehu for the blood of Jezreel. God won't have mercy on Israel, for they are no longer His people. However, Judah and Israel will one day unite as God's people with one head.

[2]**God tells Hosea to repudiate his marriage** to Gomer because of her sinfulness, for God will repudiate Israel because of its sinfulness. However, God will one day remove Israel's idolatry and will betroth them to Himself in righteousness, justice, love and mercy. [3]**God tells Hosea to redeem Gomer** and take her back, for Israel shall return to God in the latter days.

[4]There is no faithfulness or love or knowledge of God in the land of Israel. [5]God will punish Israel and Judah because of their unfaithfulness. [6]Hosea calls for Israel to return to the Lord; to press on to know Him, for He will revive them. [7]But for now, God is angry at the faithlessness of Israel and Judah. [8-9]God will punish Israel because of their sinfulness, [10]by giving them over to the king of Assyria.

[11]God has loved Israel by rescuing them from Egypt and nurturing them. However, they have continually rebelled, so they will be given over to the king of Assyria. There is still hope for Judah, because they are faithful to God. [12-13]God will punish Israel because of their sinfulness, and He

calls Judah to repent. [14]**God calls Israel to repent. God will one day heal their apostasy and they shall return to Him.**

Joel

[1]God tells Joel that Israel will be invaded by locusts and a powerful nation. The fields will be destroyed, and Israel's resources will be demolished. God calls them to gather as a people to mourn and cry out to Him.

[2]The day of the Lord is coming, when a great and powerful army of people will draw for battle. The Earth will quake and the heavens will tremble. God calls for people to repent; He will have pity on His people and He will pour out His Spirit on them. He will perform many wonders, and everyone who calls on the name of the Lord shall be saved. [3]The day of the Lord is near, when God will restore the fortunes of Judah and Jerusalem. All the nations shall be gathered together for judgement.

Amos

¹God tells Amos that He will punish Israel's neighbours, namely: Damascus, Gaza, Tyre, Edom and Ammon. ²God will punish Moab, Judah and Israel for their sinfulness. ³An adversary shall surround Israel and plunder it, ⁴for God has given Israel many warnings regarding their sin, yet they have not returned to Him.

⁵God laments over Israel and tells them to seek Him and live. Israel will suffer punishment because of their sin; the day of the Lord will be a day of darkness and gloom. God despises Israel's external solemness; He desires justice and righteousness from His people. ⁶God abhors the pride of Israel and those who dwell at ease in Jerusalem – those who indulge in luxurious comfort and ignore the plight of Israel. God will raise up a nation against them.

⁷God shows Amos visions of locusts and fire. Amos prays for forgiveness, and God promises not to deliver these. But God says that Israel will be laid waste and Jeroboam shall be killed. A priest named Amaziah tells Amos to stop prophesying, and Amos answers by saying Amaziah too will be killed and Israel will go into exile. ⁸The end is coming for Israel. There will be mourning, thirst, and a lack of hearing God's words. ⁹God is going to bring destruction upon Israel, but he will not totally destroy it. He will restore the fortunes of His people, and they will rebuild as in the days of old.

Obadiah

[1]God tells Obadiah that He will destroy Edom because of its pride and hostility towards the people of Judah. The day of the Lord is coming upon all nations. There shall be much destruction, but God's kingdom shall be a holy habitat for His people.

Jonah

[1]God tells Jonah to go and preach against a great, wicked city called Nineveh. But Jonah tries to flee from God by boarding a ship owned by pagan sailors. God sends a storm upon the sea and the sailors throw Jonah overboard. God saves Jonah by sending a great fish to swallow him up. [2]Jonah prays a prayer of contrition and praise to God whilst in the belly of the fish. After three days, the fish vomits Jonah up on dry land. [3]God tells Jonah to go to Nineveh again, and this time he does so. He preaches against it, and the whole city, including its king, believes in God and repents of their sin. God relents from bringing disaster upon them.

[4]Jonah is angry because of the grace God showed Nineveh. Jonah goes outside the city and rests. God grows a plant which gives Jonah shade, and he is pleased. But God sends a worm which destroys the plant, so Jonah becomes angry. God points out that while Jonah cares much for a plant, God cares much for the great city of Nineveh.

Micah

¹God tells Micah that He will bring destruction upon the Earth. Samaria, Israel, Jerusalem and many other regions will suffer because of their sin. ²God will bring disaster upon oppressive rulers and those who devise evil amongst His people, but He will save a faithful remnant of His people. ³God denounces the evil rulers and false prophets of Israel. Destruction is coming because of their sin.

⁴There will come a day when God's mountain shall be established, and a faithful remnant from many nations shall come and live at peace under God's word. ⁵A ruler from ancient days is going to be born in Bethlehem. He will shepherd his flock with God's strength; He shall be their peace. He shall deliver them from Assyrian forces. The remnant of Jacob shall be among the nations. God will eradicate idolatry and will destroy those who disobey Him.

⁶God appeals to Israel to know the saving acts of God, to do justice and love kindness. God will strike the wicked and make them desolate. ⁷Micah says he will look to the Lord and trust Him for salvation, despite the wickedness that surrounds him. A day is coming when the Earth will be desolate because of the sin of mankind, but God will save His people by crushing their iniquities underfoot.

Nahum

¹God speaks to a man called Nahum in a vision concerning Nineveh. God is full of wrath: He will make a complete end of His enemies, but He will save His people from slavery. ²God is restoring the majesty of Jacob, and ³He will make Nineveh desolate in the sight of the nations.

Habakkuk

[1]A prophet named Habakkuk complains that justice is perverted in the land because the wicked seem to dominate the righteous. God answers by saying He will raise up the Chaldeans to seize dwellings not their own. Habakkuk again asks why God remains silent when the wicked swallow up the righteous. [2]God answers by telling Habakkuk to wait patiently and faithfully for justice to come, for the righteous shall live by faith. God promises punishment for the wicked.

[3]Habakkuk recalls a vision of God marching through the Earth in fury, threshing the nations in anger, but providing salvation for His people. Habakkuk says that although he is afraid of foreign dangers, he will quietly wait for the day of God's justice. Though the land faces many hardships, he will rejoice in God, who alone provides salvation.

Zephaniah

[1]God tells Zephaniah that the day of the Lord is coming: a day when God will sweep away everything from the face of the Earth. He will strike Judah and Jerusalem – those who have rebelled against Him. [2]God's burning anger is coming; He will destroy Judah's enemies: Philistine, Moab, Ammon, Assyria, Nineveh and others. But God will save a faithful, righteous remnant of the house of Judah. [3]God will pour out his anger on sinful nations, but people shall come from many nations to worship Him, and He will take away their judgements. He will preserve a faithful remnant, and He will rejoice over them.

Haggai

¹God speaks to a prophet named Haggai during the times of Darius the king, Zerubbabel the governor, and Joshua the high priest. The land is experiencing famine and the temple lies in ruins. God tells them to rebuild it, and the people obey.

²The people rebuild the temple, but it doesn't seem to match the glory of the first. But God tells the people to stay strong. God will fill the temple with His glory, making it more glorious than the first. He has afflicted Israel, but from now on He will bless them. He is about to destroy the strength of the nations, and He is going to make Zerubbabel into a signet ring.

Zechariah

[1]God speaks to a prophet named Zechariah during the times of Darius the king. God calls His people to repent.

Zechariah sees a vision of a man riding on a horse, surrounded by other horses. These are patrollers of the Earth, which show that God will return to Jerusalem with mercy. Zechariah sees a vision of four horns, which are the nations which have scattered Israel, and four craftsmen, which have come to terrify Judah's enemies. [2]Zechariah sees a vision of a man with a measuring line, going to measure Jerusalem. There will come a day when God will shake the nations and punish Judah's enemies. He will dwell in the midst of His people and they shall be His portion.

[3]Zechariah sees Joshua the high priest and Satan trying to accuse him. God rebukes Satan, and gives Joshua pure clean clothes to wear – God has taken away his sin. God promises Joshua that if he obeys Him, he shall rule His house. God will send a servant – the Branch – to remove the iniquity of His people in a single day.

[4]Zechariah sees a vision of a golden lamp stand with seven lamps on it, and two olive trees by its side. God's Spirit is at work in Zerubbabel, and he will rebuild the temple. The two olive trees are the two anointed ones who stand by the Lord. [5]Zechariah sees a vision of a flying scroll, which is the curse that goes out over the land. He sees a basket, which is sin, and a woman in the basket, who is Wickedness. Two other women come and carry the basket to Babylon to build a house for it there. [6]Zechariah sees a vision of four chariots with different coloured horses, which go out to

the four winds of heaven, and patrol the Earth. Zechariah is told to make a crown for Joshua the high priest, symbolising the royalty of the Branch who will come and rebuild the temple, and will rule on his throne.

[7]Men from Bethel ask some priests a question about fasting. God says that what He truly wants is justice and mercy in the land, not self-centred fasting and ritual. [8]God will save His people from the nations and will bring them to dwell in Jerusalem, and God will be with them. They shall experience peace and prosperity.

[9]God has an eye on mankind – He will punish Israel's enemies. God's people should rejoice, for their king is coming with righteousness and salvation, mounted on a donkey. He will speak peace to the nations and will rule to the ends of the Earth. By the blood of His covenant, God will save His people.

[10]God is angry at the false shepherds and the abusive leaders in Israel. [11]God tells Zechariah to become a shepherd over a flock of sheep doomed to slaughter. He does so, but becomes impatient and gives up being a shepherd. God says he will no longer have pity on those in the land, and he pronounces woes on the worthless shepherds who desert the flock of His people.

[12]God is going to give salvation to Judah and He will destroy all the nations that come against Jerusalem. He will pour out on His people a spirit of grace, and His people shall mourn when they look at Him – the one whom they have pierced. God's people shall be cleansed from sin. [13]God will cut off idolatry, false prophecy and uncleanliness from the

land. The shepherd will be struck and the sheep will scatter. A remnant of the people shall be saved and refined, and they will be God's people.

[14]A day is coming in which God will gather all the nations against Jerusalem for battle, and it shall be plundered. Some people will go out into exile but some shall remain in the land. There is coming a day when God will be king over all the Earth and Jerusalem shall dwell in security. God will decimate those who wage war against Jerusalem, and Judah shall be restored.

Malachi

[1]God has loved the house of Jacob, but He has hated Esau. God will tear down Edom. God is a father and a master, yet the priests in Israel neither honour Him nor fear Him. They present polluted food as sacrifice upon the altar, but God will not accept this sacrifice, for His name is to be great among the nations. [2]God warns the priests saying He will curse them and their blessings because they have corrupted the covenant God made with Levi. Levi spoke the truth and walked in righteousness, but the priests have lead people astray by their instruction. Judah has been faithless; they have been idolatrous, and the men have been faithless to their wives.

[3]God will send a messenger to prepare the way for Him. The messenger of the covenant will purify God's people. God will draw near to judge Israel. They have robbed God in their tithes, and spoken against God by questioning His goodness. [4]The day is coming when God will punish evildoers and will save those who fear Him. God calls His people to remember the law that He gave Moses. God will send Elijah the prophet before the day of the Lord. He will turn the hearts of fathers to their children, and the hearts of the children to their fathers.

NEW TESTAMENT

GOSPELS

Matthew

[1]Jesus is born in Bethlehem and His genealogy is outlined. [2]Herod sends wise men to Bethlehem to find baby Jesus. They find Jesus and worship him. An angel tells Joseph to flee to Egypt with Mary and Jesus, because Herod is planning on killing Jesus. They flee, and Herod angrily kills many children in Bethlehem. Herod dies soon after, and Joseph goes to Nazareth with Mary and Jesus to settle.

[3]John the Baptist prepares the way for Jesus by preaching repentance and baptizing many. Jesus is baptized too, and the Spirit of God visibly descends upon him like a dove. [4]Jesus is tempted by the devil in the wilderness, and He resists all temptation. He then goes and begins preaching. He calls Peter, Andrew, James and John to follow Him as disciples.

[5]He goes up on a mountain and preaches a sermon about: true blessedness, being salt and light, His fulfilment of the Old Testament, anger, lust, divorce, oaths, loving your enemies, [6]humble generosity, faithful prayer, fasting, laying up for yourself treasures in heaven, anxiety, [7] not judging others, praying expectantly, treating others as you would have them treat you, the narrow gate and the hard way that leads to life, and bearing good fruit as evidence of being saved. Jesus finishes his sermon and comes down from the mountain.

[8]Jesus heals a leper, a faithful Centurion's servant, and Peter's mother-in-law. Jesus points out that following Him will involve leaving things

behind. He gets into a boat with His disciples and calms a great storm on the sea. He heals two demon-possessed men, sending the demons into a herd of pigs, which run into the sea and drown. [9]He heals a paralytic and forgives his sins. He calls Matthew the tax collector to become a disciple. He has a meal with sinners and explains why his disciples aren't fasting. He heals a bleeding woman, a ruler's daughter, two blind men, and a demon-oppressed man. He tells His disciples to pray for labourers for the harvest – shepherds for the flock of God's people. [10]He gathers His twelve disciples and prepares to send them out to proclaim the kingdom of Heaven to the lost sheep of Israel. He warns them that persecution will come, but He also tells them not to fear man.

[11]John the Baptist sends messengers to Jesus asking if He is the messiah, and Jesus confirms it. Jesus speaks to the crowds about John the Baptist. He denounces the unrepentant cities of the time, and He calls all who are heavy laden to come to Him to receive rest. [12]He claims that He is Lord of the Sabbath and heals a man with a withered hand during the Sabbath. He reveals Himself as the one spoken of in Isaiah 42:1-3. He talks about blasphemy against the Holy Spirit and about people being known by their deeds. He says that like Jonah's three days spent in a fish, He will spend three days in the heart of the Earth. He talks about who His true family is. [13]He compares different responses to God's word to different types of ground receiving seeds, and He explains why He talks in parables. He compares final judgement to a reaper separating weeds from good plants. He compares the kingdom of heaven: to a mustard seed, to leaven, to treasure hidden in a field, to a great pearl, and to a net that gathers fish of every kind. He is rejected in His hometown.

[14]Herod holds a birthday party which leads to John the Baptist being beheaded. Jesus feeds five thousand people with five loaves of bread and two fish. He walks on water and heals sick people. [15]Pharisees come to Jesus and ask Him why He breaks the traditions of the elders. Jesus rebukes them and asks them why they break God's commandments for the sake of their traditions. Jesus talks about what true defilement is, and He heals a Canaanite woman's daughter. He heals many more people, and then feeds four thousand people with seven bread loaves and a few fish. [16]The Pharisees demand a sign from Jesus, but Jesus rebukes them. He warns His disciples about the Pharisees, and He asks His disciples who people say that He is, and Peter confesses that Jesus is the Christ. Jesus says that Peter is the rock on which He will build His church. Jesus begins to speak of His coming death and resurrection in Jerusalem, and He calls for His followers to take up their crosses and follow Him.

[17]Jesus takes Peter, James and John up a mountain, and He is transfigured before them. God tells the disciples to listen to Jesus. They go down the mountain and Jesus heals a boy with a demon because the faithless disciples were not able to heal the boy themselves. Jesus foretells His death and resurrection and, while teaching a truth about tax, implies that He is the son of God. [18]Jesus uses the example of a child to teach His disciples about true greatness. He talks about the necessity to flee temptation, and He uses a parable about lost sheep to explain God's love for His children. He also uses a parable to explain why we should be forgiving others, just as God has forgiven us.

[19]Jesus talks to the Pharisees about divorce. He welcomes children to him and prays for them. He tells a rich man to sell everything he has and

to follow Him, and then He teaches the disciples about the greatness of leaving things for the sake of following Him. [20]He uses a parable involving workers who work different amounts of time but receive the same wage to explain God's freely given grace. He foretells His crucifixion and resurrection, and He tells His disciples that in order to be the greatest, they have to be servants of all.

[21]Jesus and His disciples enter Jerusalem. Jesus drives out people from the temple who were using it as a market place. He curses a fig tree and teaches His disciples about the power of faithful prayer. He tells a parable about two sons and a parable about unfaithful tenants, in order to teach about the folly of those who reject Him, as opposed to the grace that's received by those who believe in Him. [22]He uses a parable involving an open-invitation wedding feast to explain the gospel call that goes out to many. He supports paying taxes to Caesar, and He answers a question from the Sadducees about marriage. He explains the first and the second greatest commandments, and He asks the Pharisees a question about the identity of the Christ. [23]He publically pronounces woes on the hypocritical Pharisees, [24]and He talks about the close of the age. [25]He uses a parable involving ten virgins to teach about the need for God's people to be watchful and ready for Christ's return. He uses a parable involving three servants to teach about the need for God's people to be good stewards of the grace that's been given them. He talks about final judgement.

[26]A woman pours expensive ointment on Jesus in a beautiful display of adoration. Jesus spends the Passover with His disciples, and He reveals that one of them is going to betray Him. He prays in Gethsemane, before being betrayed by Judas. He is arrested and taken to a council for

judgement. Peter denies Jesus three times. [27]Judas hangs himself because he feels guilty about betraying Jesus. Jesus is taken to the Pilate the governor to be questioned. The crowd are given the option to release either Jesus or a notorious prisoner called Barabbas, and they choose Barabbas. Jesus is mocked, flogged, crucified and buried in a rich man's tomb which is protected by guards.

[28]Jesus rises from death and appears to His disciples. He commissions them to make disciples of all nations by spreading the gospel.

Mark

[1]John the Baptist prepares the way for Jesus and baptizes Him. Jesus is tempted in the wilderness and then begins His ministry in Galilee. He calls James and John to become disciples. He teaches in the synagogue and travels throughout Galilee, teaching and healing. [2]He heals a paralytic who was brought to Him by faithful friends. He calls Levi to become a disciple. He explains why His disciples don't fast, and He explains why His disciples plucked grains on the Sabbath. [3]He heals a man with a withered hand on the Sabbath, and the Pharisees start to plot how they might destroy Jesus. Jesus calls His twelve disciples (Simon, James, John, Andrew, Philip, Bartholomew, Matthew, Thomas, James, Thaddaeus, Simon and Judas) to Himself. He refutes scribes who say that He is possessed by Beelzebub, and He talks about who His true family are. [4]He uses a parable about seeds falling on different kinds of ground to explain different peoples' responses to God's word. He compares the kingdom of Heaven to a grain seed and a mustard seed. He calms a storm while on a boat with His disciples. [5]He heals a man with demons, a bleeding woman, and a synagogue-ruler's daughter.

[6]Jesus teaches in His hometown Nazareth, but He is rejected there. He gives His disciples authority over unclean spirits, and He sends them out to preach the gospel and to heal. Herod holds a birthday party which leads to John the Baptist being beheaded. The disciples return from their travels, and Jesus feeds five thousand people with five bread loaves and two fish. Jesus prays by himself, walks on water, and heals many people.

[7]Jesus rebukes the Pharisees, explaining to them that God's commandments are more important than man's traditions, and that it is what comes out of a person (sin) that defiles a person, not what goes in (food). Jesus heals a Gentile's daughter and a deaf man. [8]He feeds four thousand people with seven bread loaves and a few fish. He warns His disciples about the Pharisees and Herod. He heals another blind man and begins to speak about his coming death and resurrection.

[9]Jesus takes Peter, James and John up a mountain, and they see Jesus in a radiant, transfigured form. They go down the mountain and Jesus heals a boy with a demon because the faithless disciples were not able to heal the boy themselves. Jesus foretells His coming death and resurrection, and He uses a child to teach about true greatness. He talks about the severity of sin and the need to repent. [10]He teaches about divorce, and uses a child to illustrate how people should receive God's kingdom. He tells a rich man to sell everything he has and to follow Him, and then talks about the difficulty of entering heaven if you're wealthy. He talks about His coming death and resurrection, and teaches the disciples about servant-hood being the essence of true greatness. He heals another blind man.

[11]Jesus triumphantly enters Jerusalem on a colt. He enters the temple and drives out all the buyers and sellers who had turned the temple into a market place. He curses a fig tree and then uses it to teach His disciples about faithful prayer. The scribes ask Him a question about His authority, and He asks them a question about John the Baptist in return. [12]He speaks to the scribes and uses a parable about horrible tenants to explain the way the Prophets were treated, and how He will be treated. He talks to Pharisees about paying taxes to Caesar, and He talks to the

Sadducees about resurrection. He talks to a scribe about the most important commandments, and He warns people against following the scribes in their hypocrisy. [13]He foretells the destruction of the Temple and talks to His disciples about the end times.

[14]A woman pours expensive ointment on Jesus in a beautiful display of adoration. Jesus spends the Passover with His disciples, and He reveals that one of them is going to betray Him. Jesus prays in Gethsemane before being betrayed by Judas. He is arrested and taken to a council for judgement. Peter denies Jesus three times. [15]Jesus is taken to Pilate the governor to be questioned. The crowd are given the option to release either Jesus or a notorious prisoner called Barabbas, and they choose Barabbas. Jesus is mocked, flogged, crucified and buried in a rich man's tomb.

[16]Mary (Jesus' mother) and Mary Magdalene go to the tomb on the Sunday morning to anoint Jesus. They see an angel sitting in Jesus' tomb who tells them that Jesus is going to meet the disciples in Galilee. Jesus appears to the disciples and tells them to preach the Gospel to the whole world. Jesus ascends into Heaven and sits down at God's right hand.

Luke

[1]An angel appears to Elizabeth and Zechariah and tells them that they will have a son: John the Baptist. Another angel appears to Mary and Joseph and tells them that they will have a son: Jesus. Elizabeth gives birth to John the Baptist. [2]Mary and Joseph go to Bethlehem, and Mary gives birth to Jesus in a manger. A devout man called Simeon and a prophetess called Anna affirm Jesus as the messiah. During a festival in Jerusalem, Jesus separates from his parents and stays behind to talk to Jewish teachers, but later He goes back to Nazareth with His parents.

[3]John the Baptist prepares the way for Jesus' ministry by preaching a baptism of repentance for the forgiveness of sins, and he baptizes Jesus. [4]Jesus is tempted by the devil in the wilderness for forty days, but He does not sin. Jesus begins to teach in synagogues, but He is rejected in His hometown, Nazareth. He heals a man with a demon at Capernaum, and many others at Peter's house.

[5]Jesus calls Peter, James and John to become disciples. Jesus heals a leper and, to show that He has authority on Earth to forgive sins, heals a paralytic and forgives his sins. Jesus calls Levi to become a disciple. While celebrating at Levi's house, Jesus explains why His disciples don't fast. [6]Jesus says that He is Lord of the Sabbath, and He heals a man with a withered hand on the Sabbath. Jesus prays before choosing His twelve disciples: Peter, Andrew, James, John, Philip, Bartholomew, Matthew, Thomas, James, Simon, Judas (James' son), and Judas Iscariot. He talks to

a crowd about: true blessedness, loving your enemies, judging others, and obedience to Him.

[7]Jesus heals a centurion's servant and a widow's dead son. He confirms that He is the messiah to John the Baptist, and He talks to a crowd about John the Baptist. He forgives the sins of a sinful woman while having a meal at a proud Pharisee's house. [8]He uses a parable about seeds falling on different kinds of ground to explain different people's receptions of God's word. He calms a great storm whilst on a boat with His disciples. He heals a demon-possessed man, sending the demons into a herd of pigs, which run into the sea and drown. He heals a bleeding woman and a ruler's daughter.

[9]Jesus sends out the disciples to spread the message of the Kingdom and to heal. He feeds five thousand people with five bread loaves and two fish. He foretells His death and resurrection, and He talks about the cost of following Him. He takes Peter, James and John up a mountain, and He is transfigured before them. He heals a boy with an unclean spirit, because His disciples couldn't. He uses a child to illustrate true greatness. [10]He sends out seventy-two of His followers to proclaim the Kingdom of God. He tells a lawyer that in order to inherit eternal life, he must love God and love his neighbour. Jesus enters a house belonging to two women, Mary and Martha. Mary listens to Jesus while Martha is distracted with much serving.

[11]Jesus teaches His disciples to pray. He refutes the idea that He belongs to Satan's kingdom. He talks about the sign of Jonah being the only sign His generation shall receive. He pronounces woes on the Pharisees and the lawyers, and [12]He warns His disciples about the hypocrisy of the

Pharisees. He tells them not to fear man, but to acknowledge Christ before men. He tells them not to lay up Earthly treasures, and not to be anxious about their lives, but to be ready for Christ's second coming.

[13]Jesus, speaking to a crowd, calls all to repent and to bear fruit. He heals a woman with a disabling spirit on the Sabbath in the synagogue. He compares God's kingdom to a mustard seed, and to leaven. He calls people to enter through the narrow door into the kingdom, and He laments over Jerusalem for its unfaithfulness. [14]He dines at a ruler's house on a Sabbath. He heals a man with dropsy, He tells people not to exalt themselves, and He explains that those originally invited will not always accept the invitation, so others will be invited instead; as is the case with God's kingdom. He tells great crowds to count the cost of following Him, and He tells them that salt without saltiness is worthless.

[15]Jesus uses parables about a lost sheep, a lost coin and a prodigal son to illustrate God's joy over repentant sinners. [16]He uses a parable about a shrewd manager to illustrate how God's people should worship God and not money. He uses a parable about a rich man and a poor man called Lazarus to illustrate the sufficiency and inerrancy of scripture for salvation. [17]He talks about temptations to sin, and He says that God's people should consider themselves unworthy servants. He cleanses ten lepers, but only one praises God. He talks about the coming of the kingdom of God. [18]He uses a parable about a persistent widow to teach that God's people should always pray and not lose heart. He uses a parable involving a Pharisee and a tax collector to teach that God's people must humble themselves. He says that it is difficult for the rich to enter into heaven. He foretells His death and resurrection, and He heals a blind beggar. [19]A rich tax collector named Zacchaeus sells many of his

possessions after meeting Jesus, and Jesus says that he is saved. Nearing Jerusalem, Jesus tells a parable about three servants to teach that God's people should be faithful stewards of God's grace.

Jesus enters Jerusalem on a colt. He weeps over Jerusalem and foretells of its destruction, and He drives out entrepreneurs from the temple. [20]Scribes approach Jesus in the temple and question His authority, and in return Jesus asks them a question about John the Baptist. Jesus uses a parable about wicked tenants to teach that God is against those who reject Him. He affirms paying taxes to Caesar, and He tells Sadducees that people won't be married in heaven. He tells His disciples to beware of the Pharisees, and [21]He commends a widow's offering in the temple. He foretells the destruction of the temple and Jerusalem, and He foretells the persecution of the church. He uses a fig tree analogy to tell His disciples to be on watch for His second coming.

[22]Jesus spends the Passover with His disciples, and He reveals that one of them is going to betray Him. He establishes the Lord's Supper. He deals with the disciples' query of who will be the greatest. He prays in Gethsemane before being betrayed by Judas. He is arrested and taken to a council for judgement. Peter denies Him three times. [23]The council sends Him to Pilate, who sends Him to Herod, who sends Him back to Pilate. The crowd are given the option to release either Jesus or a notorious prisoner called Barabbas, and they choose Barabbas. Jesus is crucified and buried in a rich man's tomb.

[24]Jesus rises from death. Women find the tomb empty, and they tell the disciples, but they don't believe it. Jesus appears to two disciples on a road near Jerusalem. He interprets to them all the scriptures concerning

Himself. He later appears to the eleven disciples and does the same with them. He promises that the Holy Spirit will come upon them, and He ascends back into heaven.

John

[1]Jesus is the Word, and He is God, and He is coming into the world. John the Baptist admits that he himself is not the messiah, but he is preparing the way for the messiah. Jesus comes to John the Baptist for baptism, and the Spirit descends on Jesus like a dove. Jesus calls Andrew, Peter, Philip, Nathaniel and another person to become disciples.

[2]Jesus attends a wedding in Galilee and turns water into wine.

He goes to Jerusalem and drives out the entrepreneurs from the temple. [3]A Pharisee named Nicodemus meets Jesus and acknowledges Him as a teacher from God. Jesus says to him that he has to be born again; He must believe in Him for salvation. Jesus and His disciples baptize people in the Judean country side, and someone approaches John the Baptist and tells him that all are going to Jesus. John the Baptist says that he must decrease, and that Jesus must increase.

[4]Jesus talks to a Samaritan woman at a well and tells her that He is the Christ. Many Samaritans believe in Jesus. He heals an Official's son.

[5]He goes to a healing pool in Jerusalem and heals a man who can't walk. Jesus calls Himself the Son of Man and says that God has delegated judgement to Him. He says that in Him is life, and that the scriptures bear witness about Him. [6]He feeds five thousand people with five bread loaves and two fish, and He walks on water. He calls Himself the 'bread of life', and calls His words 'spirit and life'. He says that whoever comes

to Him, believes in Him and feeds on Him, will not die but have eternal life.

[7]Jesus secretly goes to the Feast of Booths in Judea and teaches in the Temple, telling people that He speaks on God's authority for God's glory, and that anyone who thirsts can come to Him to drink and be satisfied. He tells people to judge with right judgement, and some people question whether Jesus is the Christ. [8]The Pharisees bring an adulterer to Jesus, but He doesn't condemn her, but tells her to go and sin no more. Jesus calls Himself the light of the world, and calls people to follow Him. He says to abide in God's word, for the truth will set people free. He says that the reason why people don't believe in Him is because they are not of God; He is not their father.

[9]Jesus leaves the Temple and heals a man born blind. The Pharisees question the blind man as to what happened, but the blind man doesn't give them the answers they want, so they reject him. [10]Jesus uses a parable about sheep and a shepherd to explain His relationship with His people – Jesus is the good shepherd. Jesus says that no one is able to snatch His sheep out of His hand or the Father's hand; Jesus and the Father are one.

[11]Lazarus, brother of Mary and Martha, dies. Jesus goes to Bethany and is met by Martha, and He tells her that He is the resurrection and the life. Mary comes weeping, and Jesus weeps, and they go to the tomb of Lazarus. Jesus raises Lazarus from death. [12]Jesus has dinner at the house of Mary, Martha and Lazarus, and Mary pours expensive ointment on Jesus.

Jesus enters Jerusalem on a donkey. Some Greeks seek Jesus, and Jesus says that whoever loves his life loses it. Jesus says that He must be lifted up, and that He has come to save the world.

[13]During a supper, Jesus washes His disciples' feet, giving them an example of humility to follow. He foretells that Judas will betray Him. He tells His disciples to love one another, and He predicts that Peter will deny Him three times. [14]He says that He will leave, but He will come back for His disciples. He calls Himself the way, the truth and the life. He promises that a Helper will come for the disciples once He goes, and He says that those who love Him will keep His word. [15]He calls Himself the vine and His people the branches. He calls His disciples to abide in Him, in order that they may bear much fruit, so that God might be glorified. He talks about why the world hates Him and His disciples. [16]He talks about the work of the Helper that will come when He leaves. He says that the disciples will be sorrowful when He leaves, but their sorrow will turn to joy when they see Him again. He foretells that the disciples will scatter when He leaves, and He tells His disciples not to worry, because He has overcome the world.

[17]Jesus asks God to glorify Him in order that God would be glorified. Jesus prays that God would keep His people in His name, that they may be one in the faith and in sanctification. [18]Jesus goes with His disciples to the garden of Gethsemane, but they are met by Judas and a band of soldiers who take Jesus away to be questioned by the high priest. Peter denies Jesus three times. Jesus is sent to Pilate, who questions Him. Pilate gives the Jews the option to release either Jesus or a criminal called Barabbas, and the crowd choose to release Barabbas. [19]Jesus is mocked, flogged, crucified, and buried in a rich man's tomb.

[20]Three days later, Jesus rises from death and appears to Mary Magdalene and the disciples. The purpose of the book of John is outlined: that we may believe that Jesus is the Christ and that we may have life in His name. [21]Jesus appears to the disciples again while they're fishing, and because of Him they're able to catch a lot of fish. Jesus asks Peter if he loves Him, and three times Peter says yes.

Acts

¹Jesus' promise of the Holy Spirit and His ascension are recounted. Judas' death is recounted, and Matthias is chosen to fill his spot as one of the twelve apostles.

²The Holy Spirit comes to the Apostles, and they speak in various tongues. Peter addresses all who live in Judea, and tells them to let all Israel know that God has made Jesus both Lord and Christ. Peter calls all to be baptized for the forgiveness of sins. God continues to grow the number of believers.

³Peter and John go to the Temple and heal a lame beggar there. Peter addresses all the people in Solomon's Portico, and tells them to repent that their sins may be blotted out. ⁴Priests and Sadducees arrest Peter and John and tell them to stop speaking in the name of Jesus. Peter and John reply that they cannot stop speaking about Jesus. They are released, and they go to their friends, and they pray for boldness. God continues to grow the number of believers.

⁵A married couple, Ananias and Sapphira, lie about their offerings, and they die.

The high priest and the Sadducees put the Apostles in prison. An angel of the Lord releases them from prison, and they go and preach in the temple. The Apostles are brought before a council and they are told not to speak in the name of Jesus. The Apostles refuse to stop speaking about Jesus. They are released, and they continue to preach. ⁶The Apostles delegate some financial responsibilities to seven faithful men.

A faithful man called Steven is falsely accused of blasphemy, and he is brought before a council. ⁷Stephen gives his defence before the council: he recounts the history of Abraham and Moses, and he accuses those present of being stiff-necked. Those present stone him to death. ⁸A Pharisee called Saul persecutes the church in Jerusalem. Philip, one of the disciples, proclaims the gospel to residents in Samaria, to a magician called Simon, and to an Ethiopian eunuch.

⁹Saul is blinded and spoken to by Jesus, who tells Saul to go to Damascus and await further instruction. God sends a man called Ananias to Saul to lay hands on him, and Saul puts his faith in God. Saul joins the apostles and the disciples in Jerusalem and starts preaching there. He then goes to Tarsus.

Peter heals a paralysed man in Lydda and a dead girl in Joppa. ¹⁰A gentile called Cornelius from Caesarea has a vision which tells him to send men to bring Peter to him. Peter has a vision where he is told by God to eat food that is traditionally unclean. Cornelius's men bring Peter to him, and Peter tells Cornelius and other gentiles the gospel, and they put their faith in Jesus. ¹¹Peter goes to Jerusalem and tells the disciples about bringing the gospel to the gentiles.

Some Christians preach the gospel in Antioch, and Barnabas and Saul go there to preach.

[12]Herod, the king, kills James, a disciple of Jesus, and arrests Peter. An angel of the Lord appears and rescues Peter from prison. Peter goes to Mary's house, where many were praying, to tell them what had happened. Herod dies.

[13]Saul (now Paul) and Barnabas are sent out by the Holy Spirit, and they go and preach the gospel in Cyprus and Pisidia. Paul preaches the gospel in a synagogue in Pisidia and many believe, but devout Jews drive them out of the district. [14]Paul and Barnabas go to Iconium, Lystra and Derbe to preach the gospel. In Lystra, they are thought to be gods, and Paul is stoned and dragged out of the city. Paul, not dead, wakes up and re-enters the city. They move on to Derbe and preach the gospel, and then they travel back to Antioch in Syria. [15]False teachers start to teach that you need circumcision to be saved. The Apostles meet and agree that people are saved through the grace of Jesus. Paul and Barnabas bring a letter to the gentiles in Antioch which encourages them to abstain from four traditionally impure things. Paul and Barnabas separate: Paul takes Silas and goes to Syria, while Barnabas takes Mark and goes to Cyprus.

[16]Paul and Silas are joined by a Jewish boy named Timothy. Paul has a vision telling him to go to Macedonia, so they go. Paul casts a demon out of a girl, but this disables her fortune-telling abilities, so her parents seize Paul and the others and put them in prison. An earthquake allows them to escape, but they stay and talk to the prison jailer, who puts his faith in God. [17]Paul, Silas and Timothy go to Thessalonica and preach the gospel, and are persecuted by devout Jews. Silas and Timothy stay there, but Paul goes to Athens, a place full of idols, and teaches the men there about the one true God.

[18]Paul goes and preaches in Corinth, and meets a fellow Jewish tent-maker named Aquila. After heavy Jewish persecution, Paul returns to Antioch. A Jew named Apollos preaches in Ephesus, and he is further trained in the scriptures by Aquila and his wife Priscilla. [19]Paul goes to Ephesus and preaches. A riot breaks out because Paul says that man-made gods are not gods at all, and this threatens the man-made gods of the Ephesians. [20]Paul goes to Macedonia and Greece to preach. In Troas, a young man falls asleep while listening to Paul, and falls out of a window, but Paul heals him. Paul visits the Ephesian elders and admonishes them in their ministry.

[21]Paul, against the advice of some of his brothers, goes to Jerusalem. Paul visits James and encourages him. Paul goes into the temple, but some Jews see him and accuse him of defiling the temple. They try to kill him, but soldiers intervene and try to take Paul into the barracks to be safe. [22]Paul stops and faces the crowd and gives a short speech recounting his conversion and calling to preach to the gentiles. When they hear this, the crowd is further angered, so Paul is taken away to be flogged. However, on hearing that Paul is a Roman citizen, they instead bring him before a council for questioning. [23]Paul, before the council, speaks of the resurrection, which causes a violent division between the Pharisees and Sadducees. Paul is taken to the barracks for safety, and at night God appears to him and tells him that he will be a witness in Rome. A plot to kill Paul is thwarted by his nephew, and Paul is taken to Caesarea, to the Governor, Felix, for questioning. [24]The Jews accuse Paul of stirring up all the Jews throughout the world, and Paul defends himself. Paul is kept in prison for two years, and then Felix is succeeded by Porcius Festus, while Paul is left in prison. [25]The Jews accuse Paul once again, but this time before Governor Festus. Paul appeals to Caesar,

and Festus tells him that he shall go to Caesar. A king named Agrippa, who rules over several gentile territories, comes to greet Festus. He hears about Paul and wants to hear his case, so a trial is set up involving Paul, Festus, the Jews, and king Agrippa. [26]Paul gives his defence before Agrippa, telling him about his conversion. Agrippa finds no grounds for putting Paul to death. But, because Paul had appealed to Caesar, Paul will now go to Rome to give his appeal before Caesar.

[27]Paul is put on a ship headed for Rome. After a fortnight of bad weather, the ship wrecks off the island of Malta. The crew, mainly fellow prisoners, swim safely to land. [28]The natives at Malta treat the prisoners kindly, and Paul heals their sick. After three months, they set sail on another ship and arrive in Rome. In Rome, Paul meets with the Jewish elders and tells them about Jesus. Some believe, and some don't. Paul lives in Rome for two years, welcoming all who come to him, proclaiming the gospel with all boldness.

NEW TESTAMENT

EPISTLES

Romans

[1]Paul wants to go to Rome to preach the gospel, because those who put their faith in Jesus will be counted righteous and will be saved, but the unrighteous shall be subject to God's wrath. [2]God's judgement rightly falls on those who practice evil, while those who obey God will be justified. [3]No one obeys God perfectly; all are under sin. Therefore, no one can be saved by works of the law. However, God sent Jesus as a propitiation for our sin, so that we can be justified by God's grace as a gift, by putting our faith in Jesus. [4]Faith was counted to Abraham as righteousness, and those who put their faith in Jesus will be counted as righteous. [5]Christ died for the ungodly, so now we have peace with God. Adam's sin brought condemnation, but Jesus' sacrifice leads to justification and life.

[6]God's people shouldn't continue in sin. Because of Jesus' death and resurrection, Christians should consider themselves dead to sin and alive to God; free from sin and slaves to righteousness. [7]The law is good in that it conveys God's commands, but it is not enough for salvation because sinful people can't obey the law. Christians no longer serve in the old way of the written law, but they serve in the new way of the Spirit. [8]Christians have the Holy Spirit living in them. Jesus died so that the righteous requirement might be fulfilled for Christians, who are now sons of God and heirs of God with Christ, provided we suffer with Him, and by the Spirit put sin to death. The Spirit helps us in our weakness, and nothing can separate us from the love of Christ.

[9]God predestines those He saves. This predestination is not based on man's works, but on God's will. He rightfully does this: He is the creator; He can do what He wants. In not saving some, He makes known the riches of His glory to those He saves. Righteousness comes through faith, both for Jew and Gentile; [10]everyone who puts their faith in Jesus will be saved. [11]While not all Israelites (by descent) have put their faith in Jesus, this doesn't mean God hasn't kept His promises to Abraham; God has not rejected those whom He foreknew. Through Israel's trespass, salvation has been offered to the Gentiles. God has consigned disobedience to all, so that He may show mercy to all without distinction. God is severe towards those who don't have faith in Him, but kind to those who do.

[12]Christians are to present themselves as living sacrifices by being transformed by the renewal of their minds, so that they may discern and do what is good, becoming more like Jesus in every way. [13]Christians are to be subject to the governing authorities. Christians are to pay to all what is owed to them, love their neighbour as themselves, and put sin to death. [14]Christians are to be humble; not judging others or being a hindrance to others, but aiming for mutual encouragement, doing everything by faith in Jesus. [15]Christians are to imitate Christ in bearing with one another for the glory of God. Christ brings hope to both Jew and Gentile. Paul is a minister to the Gentiles, and hopes to come to Rome soon. [16]Paul wants the Romans to be wise as to what is good, and innocent as to what is evil, to the glory of God.

1 Corinthians

[1]Paul is thankful that God has shown the Corinthians grace in Jesus Christ. Paul wants there to be no division among the Corinthians. Paul wants them to be united in keeping Christ crucified the centre of all they do and teach.

[2]Paul keeps Christ crucified the centre of all he does and teaches. Jesus is the wisdom of God, revealed to us through the Holy Spirit, whom we have received to teach us about Jesus. [3]Paul is concerned that the Corinthians are still of the flesh, for there is still jealousy and division among them. Paul reminds the Corinthians that he has laid the foundation by preaching Christ crucified, and those who build upon that foundation must do so in such a way that keeps Christ the centre. [4]God's people are servants of Christ and stewards of the gospel. God has given Christians everything in Christ, making them rich. But at the same time Christians are the scum of the world, because to the world Christ is folly. Paul admonishes the Corinthians to know this, to trust in God, and to be faithful in Christ.

[5]Paul addresses the fact that there is sexual immorality among the Corinthians. Paul calls for the Corinthians to repent of their arrogant boasting, their malice and their evil, and to celebrate in sincerity and truth the fact that Christ has been sacrificed for them. [6]Paul warns the Corinthians that the unrighteous will not inherit God's kingdom. He tells them to flee sexual immorality, and tells them to glorify God in their bodies. [7]Paul gives the Corinthians some principles for marriage;

principles that aim to minimise anxiety and secure undivided devotion to God. Paul tells the Corinthians to live as they were called, while keeping the commandments of God. [8]What we eat doesn't make us right with God. Christians ought to love God, and not cause others to stumble. [9]They are to endure anything, give up everything, become a servant to all – doing everything it takes to preach the gospel.

[10]Paul tells the Corinthians to consider Israel, and to learn from their mistakes. Paul tells the Corinthians to flee from idolatry, and live for the glory of God, who is faithful in granting salvation to His people. [11]Paul tells the Corinthians to honour God and remember His acts of creation when participating in the tradition of head coverings. Paul exhorts the Corinthians to love one another, remember Christ's death, and honour God when participating in the Lord's Supper. [12]Paul tells the Corinthians to use their spiritual gifts in such a way as to build up and serve the body of Christ, the church. [13]Everything Christians do should be undergirded by love for God and love for others. [14]Paul tells the Corinthians to use their gifts, such as prophecy, in an orderly manner and for this purpose: to build up the church of Christ. [15]Paul reaffirms the centrality of the gospel and reassures the Corinthians that Christ was indeed raised from death, and is now alive. Christians too will die, but they will be raised. [16]Paul tells the Corinthians of his plans to visit them, and he gives them his final greetings.

2 Corinthians

[1]Paul tells the Corinthians of his sufferings as a Christian, and the comfort he finds in Christ. Paul tells them that although he planned to visit them a second time, he has refrained from doing so. [2]Paul writes to make sure the Corinthians are being obedient in everything: proclaiming Christ in all sincerity.

[3]By God's grace, we are made competent to be ministers of a new, more glorious covenant. By the Spirit we have an unbreakable hope, therefore we are bold. By the Spirit we are being made more like Jesus. [4]In weakness and affliction we preach the gospel, and it is God who powerfully saves people. While we suffer now, there is an eternal weight of glory that is ours in Christ. [5]Our gospel convictions drive our actions. We live in the world now, but God an eternal home prepared for us. Therefore we are courageous and faithful.

[6]Paul calls the Corinthians to widen their hearts. He tells them be holy as a church; to not be unequally yoked with unbelievers. [7]Paul recounts his trip to Macedonia, the coming of Titus, and his first letter that he wrote to the Corinthians, which made them grieve with a godly grief which has produced a repentance that leads to salvation. Paul has perfect confidence in the Corinthians. [8]He tells of the generosity of the churches of Macedonia, and encourages the Corinthians to also be generous. He tells them that Titus is coming to visit them. [9]He encourages the Corinthians to make ready a financial gift for the suffering Christians in Jerusalem. He reminds them that God loves a cheerful giver, and that

they will be enriched in every way to be generous in every way, to the glory of God.

[10]Paul defends his ministry, reminding the Corinthians that while he isn't physically powerful or rhetorically impressive, he preaches the gospel faithfully. [11]He warns the Corinthians against being deceived by false teachers. He tells of his extensive persecutions as a Christian, and his impressive qualifications as a Jew. However, he says that he will boast in what highlights his weakness, namely, the death and resurrection of Jesus. [12]Paul says that God's strength is magnified in human weakness, and that is why he is content in weakness for the sake of Christ. Paul is worried that many Corinthians might not repent, and [13]He calls the Corinthians to examine themselves to see whether they are in the faith. He gives his final warnings and greetings.

Galatians

[1]Paul is concerned that the Galatians are listening to false teachers who are distorting the gospel. He assures them that the gospel is not a human fabrication, but a divine message of salvation. [2]He recounts how he himself was faced with false teachers, but he did not submit to them but maintained that salvation is by grace alone; by faith in Jesus and not by works of the law. [3]He rebukes the Galatians, saying that those who rely on works of the law won't be saved, but those who put their faith in Jesus will be saved. Just as Abraham's faith was counted as righteousness, so our faith is counted as righteousness.

[4]In Christ we are no longer slaves to sin but sons of God and heirs through God. Paul is perplexed that the Galatians would even consider returning to the worthless false teachings of works-based righteousness. [5]He warns the Galatians that Christ is no advantage to those who put their faith in circumcision and other works of the law for righteousness. He tells the Corinthians to put their faith in Jesus, and to walk by the Spirit. [6]He exhorts the Galatians to bear one another's burdens, and to persevere in doing good. He tells the Galatians not to boast in their flesh, but to boast and trust in Jesus, in whom we have salvation.

Ephesians

[1]Paul thanks God because in Christ He has adopted us as sons, redeemed us through His blood, given us an inheritance, and sealed us with the Holy Spirit. Paul prays that God would grow the Ephesians in the knowledge of Him; in the knowledge of who God is and what He has done.

[2]We were dead in our sins, but our merciful God has made us alive with Christ. This salvation is by grace through faith – not of works. All who are under this grace have been made one in Christ; nobody is separated. [3]Paul wants all to know the mystery of the gospel: that in Christ, everyone – Jews and Gentiles – are partakers in salvation through faith. Paul prays that the Ephesians might know the love of Christ, and have Christ dwell in their hearts through faith.

[4]In light of Christ's love, Paul urges the Ephesians to repent of sin and to be renewed in the spirit of their minds; to put off the old self and to put on the new self. God gracefully equips the saints for the work of ministry and the building up of the church. [5]Paul urges the Ephesians to walk in love, imitating Christ. He calls them to put off sin and to be holy. He calls wives to submit to their husbands, and he calls for husbands to love their wives. [6]He calls for children to obey their parents, and slaves to obey their masters. He urges all to be strong in the Lord, and to put on the whole armour of God – truth, righteousness, gospel-readiness, faith, salvation, and the word of God. He urges all to pray fervently, and he asks people to pray for him as well.

Philippians

[1]Paul thanks God for the Philippians and their partnership in the gospel. Paul, now in prison, tells them that whether by life or by death, he aims to honour Christ. He encourages the Philippians to live a life worthy of the gospel. [2]He encourages the Philippians to consider the humility of Jesus, and to imitate Him in full accord and with one mind. He expresses his desire to send Timothy and Epaphroditus to the Philippians.

[3]Paul encourages the Philippians to rejoice in the Lord Jesus, whose worth surpasses everything else, and who brings about righteousness for those who put their faith in Him. Paul encourages them to press on towards the goal, persevering in their faith, holding firm the truth of the gospel. [4]Paul encourages the Philippians again to rejoice in the Lord, and to trust God in everything through prayer. Paul tells the Philippians to think and act in such a way that honours God, who is sovereign and provides for His people.

Colossians

[1]Paul thanks God for the Colossians and their faith in Christ. Paul prays that they would grow in the knowledge of Christ so as to walk in a manner worthy of the Lord Jesus, who is preeminent in all things, and who died to reconcile us back to Himself. Pauls toils to proclaim Christ wholeheartedly. [2]He exhorts the Colossians to remain firm in their faith in Christ, who triumphs over evil and who makes us alive in Him even though we were dead in sin. Paul warns the Colossians against submitting to false teachings of works-based righteousness, and tells them to remain in Christ through faith.

[3]Paul encourages the Colossians to set their minds on things above; to put off sin and to put on Christ in thankfulness. Paul instructs wives, husbands, slaves and masters to act in such a way that honours God. [4]Paul encourages the Colossians to continue in prayer, and to pray for him.

1 Thessalonians

[1]Paul thanks God for the Thessalonians and their faith in Christ. The Thessalonians' faith is obvious, and has had a positive impact on all the saints in Macedonia.

[2]Paul reminds the Thessalonians of his initial ministry to them; how he faithfully shared the gospel with them. He tells the Thessalonians that it wasn't in vain, for they received the gospel as God's word and have become imitators of Christ, even suffering for the sake of the gospel. [3]Paul wanted to visit the Thessalonians, but Satan hindered his coming. Therefore Paul sent Timothy, who established and exhorted them in their faith, and then reported to Paul the comforting news of the Thessalonians' faithfulness. Paul prays that they would continue to increase in faith and love.

[4]Paul urges the Thessalonians to continue in sanctification; to continue in living for God, more and more. Paul encourages them by assuring them that those who die, if they have their faith in Christ, will rise to everlasting life. [5]Paul speaks about the end times, and calls the Thessalonians to be sober and ready in faith, love and hope. He tells them to hold fast what is good and to abstain from evil. He tells them to pray without ceasing, and to pray for him as well.

2 Thessalonians

[1]Paul thanks God for the Thessalonians and their increasing faith and love in Christ. Paul talks about God's righteous judgement; God's punishment of the wicked and vindication of the righteous. Paul prays that God would continue to sanctify the Thessalonians, so that Jesus would be glorified in them.

[2]Paul speaks of the end times, and says that the "rebellion comes first" and the "man of lawlessness is revealed" before God's final judgement. Paul thanks God for choosing the Thessalonians as first fruits for salvation. He tells them to stand firm in their faith, and [3]he asks them to pray for him and his companions. He exhorts them to abstain from idleness, and he tells them to not grow weary in doing good.

1 Timothy

[1]Paul urges Timothy to stay in Ephesus, to preach the gospel faithfully and to speak out against false teaching. Paul thanks God for Jesus, who came into the world to save sinners, and for his appointment to the ministry of the gospel.

[2]Paul urges that prayer be made for all people. He gives instructions to women in regards to their role in upholding purity and in the running of the church. [3]He outlines the qualifications for overseers and deacons. He hopes to come soon to Timothy in Ephesus, but he writes so that if he delays, Timothy would know how people should behave in the church, which is rooted and built up in the gospel of Christ.

[4]Paul exhorts Timothy to speak out against false teaching, and to make sure that his own teaching is truth. [5]Paul gives Timothy instructions as to how to treat older men, younger men, older women, younger women, widows, elders, and slaves. [6]Paul urges Timothy to flee from false teachings and to preach the gospel faithfully. Paul talks about contentment and the danger of riches.

2 Timothy

¹Paul thanks God for Timothy, who has his faith in Jesus. Paul tells Timothy not to be ashamed of the gospel, but to guard it by proclaiming it truthfully, and suffering for the sake of it. ²Paul tells Timothy to remember Jesus, and to share in His suffering. Paul calls Timothy to avoid false teaching, and to speak the truth of the gospel. Paul tells Timothy to flee sin and pursue what Christ has called him to.

³Paul tells Timothy that evil people will go on from bad to worse, and that there will be godlessness in the last days. Paul calls Timothy to live a Godly life and to persevere in preaching God's word, which is breathed out by God and able to make us competent; equipped for every good work. ⁴Paul charges Timothy to preach the word of God. He charges him to be sober-minded and to endure suffering.

Titus

[1]Paul writes to Titus, whom Paul left at Crete to organise what remained of their church. Paul outlines the qualifications for elders/overseers. Paul tells him to sharply rebuke false teachers, and [2]to preach sound doctrine. Paul outlines how older men, older women, younger women, younger men, and slaves, should all behave. He talks about the grace of God – Jesus – bringing us all salvation and training us to renounce sin as we await His second coming.

[3]Paul reminds Titus that we were once foolish; dead in sin. But when our saviour Jesus appeared, He saved us, not because of our works, but because of His own mercy. We have been made new by the Holy Spirit, so that we can be heirs according to the hope of eternal life. In light of this, Paul tells Titus to tell everyone to devote themselves to good works, holding fast the word of God.

Philemon

[1]Paul thanks God for Philemon, who has his faith in Christ as he works to spread the gospel. Paul appeals to Philemon to welcome Onesimus, who is like a son and a brother to Paul, and who Paul is sending to serve with Philemon in his ministry. Paul wants to visit Philemon, and he asks him to pray for his arrival.

Hebrews

[1]The author speaks of God revealing Himself through Jesus. Jesus is God and has made purification for sins, and He is superior to angels. [2]Jesus is perfect, and He died to save those who are slaves to the fear of death. He suffered when tempted so that He can help those who are being tempted. He is the founder of salvation, so we can't neglect Him, but rather we must pay much closer attention to Him. [3]Consider Jesus, who is worthy of more glory than Moses, and hold fast your confidence in Him. Don't harden your heart, but exhort each other daily, that none of you may be hardened by the deceitfulness of sin.

[4]The promise of entering God's rest still stands. We must strive to enter that rest by holding fast our confession about Jesus, who is able to sympathise with us in our weaknesses, and whom we can approach at any time for mercy and help. [5]Jesus is a greater High Priest, for He was appointed by God and He was made perfect through suffering. We must move on from being infants; unskilled in God's word, and we must become mature; able to discern between good and evil. [6]We must be mature in our faith and teaching, and we must hold onto God's certain promise by faith and patience.

[7]Melchizedek was both a king and a priest during the time of Abraham. No beginning or end is recorded of him. However, Jesus is greater than Melchizedek. Jesus holds His priesthood eternally by an irrevocable oath of God. Jesus introduces us to a better hope and a better covenant through which we draw near to God. He is holy, innocent, unstained, and

He offered himself as a one-time sacrifice for all. [8]Jesus is High Priest of a better covenant; one which is enacted on better promises, where God writes His word on His people's hearts, His people all know Him, and He forgives them of all sin.

[9]The old covenant, involving animal's blood being continually sacrificed in the Earthly holy place by sinful intercessory High Priests, was not sufficient for salvation. Jesus is the mediator of a new covenant, involving Jesus' blood being shed once to bring about salvation for all who put their faith in Him, and Jesus acting as a faithful intercessory High Priest for us in heaven. [10]Jesus died once for all. Let us therefore draw near to God with a true heart in full assurance of faith, with our hearts sprinkled clean from an evil conscience and our bodies washed with pure water. Let us put off sin and hold onto the confidence we have in Jesus.

[11]Faith is the conviction of things not seen. By faith the people of old received their commendation. Abel, Enoch, Noah, Abraham, Sarah, Isaac, Jacob, Joseph, Moses, Rahab, and many others, were accepted by God on the basis of faith. [12]Since we are surrounded by so many faithful witnesses from the past, let us put sin to death and run the race of faith, looking to Jesus, who founded and perfects our faith, and who endured suffering for our sake. Let us endure like Jesus did, and let us be grateful that Jesus gives us a kingdom that cannot be shaken. [13]Keep looking to Jesus and keep seeking the Kingdom that is to come. Become more like Jesus in your actions and acknowledge Jesus in everything. The author asks the Hebrews to pray for him and his brothers.

James

[1]James writes to Christians in the Dispersion, exhorting them to rejoice and persevere in trial and testing. He talks about the exaltation of the lowly and the humiliation of the rich. He calls Christians everywhere to put away sin and to receive, obey and live out God's word.

[2]James exhorts the Christians to show no partiality; to treat the rich and the poor equally, without favouritism. James says that faith that is not accompanied by works is dead. [3]He talks about the danger of the tongue and its potential to both build up and destroy. He talks about wisdom from above which leads to peace and a harvest of righteousness. [4]He warns against friendship with the world, which is enmity with God, and calls all to repent of worldliness and to draw near to God in humility, attributing to Him sovereignty in all things. [5]He warns those who live in self-indulgence, and encourages Christians to patiently and faithfully wait for Jesus' second coming. He exhorts all Christians to pray fervently for all needs.

1 Peter

[1]Peter writes to Christians in the Dispersion, reminding them that they have been born again to a living hope through Jesus' death and resurrection. Peter encourages them to set their hope fully on the grace of God, and to be holy in all their conduct.

[2]As we come to Jesus, the living stone, we ourselves like living stones are being built up as a spiritual house; a holy priesthood, that we may proclaim the gospel of Christ. We are to abstain from sin and follow Jesus – obeying authorities, loving our brothers and sisters in Christ, and fearing God. [3]Peter gives instructions to wives and husbands, and calls all to strive for unity with humble minds and tender hearts, following Christ in all things. Peter talks about suffering and relating to those who are opposed to Jesus. He talks of Jesus' suffering for our salvation, and His resurrection from death.

[4]We are to live for the rest of time no longer for human passions but for the will of God. We are to rejoice in sharing Christ's sufferings, entrusting ourselves to our faithful Creator whilst doing good.

[5]Peter exhorts the elders to shepherd the flock of God as examples to the flock. He tells those who are younger to be subject to the elders. He tells all to be humble; fervent in prayer, and to resist the devil, firm in faith, trusting God in all things, standing firm in the true grace of God.

2 Peter

[1]Through faith, Christians partake of the divine nature and escape the corruption that is in the world due to sin. We are to supplement our faith with virtue, knowledge, self-control, steadfastness, godliness, brotherly affection and love. In practicing these qualities and bearing good fruit, we make our election sure. We know the power and majesty of Jesus through the prophetic word which comes from God.

[2]Peter talks about false prophets and [3]calls Christians to hold fast the Word of God, living lives of holiness as they wait patiently for the day of the Lord. We are to abstain from sin and grow in the grace and knowledge of our Lord Jesus Christ.

1 John

[1]Jesus is the word of life and He brings about eternal life. God is light, and Christians must walk in the light so that they might have joyous fellowship with one another, and so that Jesus would cleanse them from all sin. [2]Jesus is our advocate — we can find forgiveness in Him when we sin. We may know that we are in Christ by keeping His commandments. We must not love the world or the things of the world, but we must let what we've learned about Jesus abide in us, and cling to Jesus as our Lord and saviour.

[3]We must continually remember that God has loved us and called us His children, and we must hope in Him. Everyone who makes a practice of sinning is not in Jesus. We must love one another, looking to Jesus, for by His sacrifice on the cross we truly know what love is. [4]We must be careful when listening to teachers/spirits, for if they do not confess that Jesus is Lord then they are false. In light of God's love for us and His sending Jesus to die for us, we should love others.

[5]Jesus is the true God and eternal life. In light of this, we must love God and obey His commandments, knowing that we have eternal life in Jesus' name, and praying to God for anything we need.

2 John

[1]John rejoices at the fact that some of his recipients are walking in the truth. John exhorts them to strive to love one another by walking according to the commandments. John urges them to abide in the true word of God, and to reject false teaching.

3 John

[1]John writes to a faithful brother in Christ, Gaius, who is walking in the truth and teaching the truth. John encourages Gaius to support faithful brothers, and to imitate good and resist evil. John wishes to address his concerns about Diotrephes, who rejects John's authority and who refuses to welcome the faithful brothers. John says he will come and visit Gaius soon.

Jude

[1]Jude writes to Christians, warning them against false teachers who distort the gospel. Jude calls them to persevere in the truth, praying fervently, keeping themselves in God's love while showing mercy to others.

Revelation

[1]John receives a revelation of Jesus Christ from God through an angel while on the island on Patmos. The revelation regards the end times, when Jesus will come back in glory.

[2]John is told to write to the churches of Ephesus, Smyrna, Pergamum, Thyatira, [3]Sardis, Philadelphia, and Laodicea – to encourage their faith and call them to repent of sin.

[4]John sees a vision of God seated on a throne, surrounded by twenty-four elders each on a throne, along with four living creatures. They all worship God and give Him glory. [5]God holds a scroll in His hand, with seven seals, but no one is found worthy to open the scroll. However, Jesus – the lion of Judah, the Root of David, the lamb that was slain – takes the scroll to open it. All the elders and all the angels and all of creation worship Jesus and give Him glory. [6]The first six seals are opened by the lamb (Jesus). As the seals are opened, wrath and destruction come upon the Earth. [7]All God's people, from every nation and tongue are sealed; brought before the throne of God in white robes, where they worship God and the lamb (Jesus), and joyfully give Him glory day and night.

[8]An angel with a golden censer is given incense to offer with the prayers of all the saints to God. Seven angels, each with a trumpet, stand before God's throne. The first four blow their trumpets, and destruction comes upon the Earth. [9]The next two angels blow their trumpets, and more

destruction comes upon the Earth. [10]A mighty angel comes down from heaven with a little scroll in his hand, and he gives it to John to eat, and it is bitter-sweet. The angel says that when the seventh trumpet is blown, the mystery of God will be fulfilled. [11]God says He will have two witnesses who will prophesy and have authority to inflict wrath on the Earth. However, the beast from the bottomless pit will kill the witnesses, but God will raise them back to life about three days later. The seventh angel blows his trumpet, and voices in heaven worship God, as the kingdom of the world becomes God's kingdom. More destruction falls on the Earth.

[12]John sees a pregnant woman and a great red dragon (Satan). The woman gives birth to a male child, who is to rule the nations, and the dragon looks to devour the child, but the child is caught up to God and His throne. Michael and his angels fight the dragon in heaven, and the dragon is thrown down to Earth. The dragon pursues the woman, but can't defeat her, so he goes after her offspring (the church). [13]John sees a beast rising out of the sea, which teams up with the dragon to blaspheme against God and lead the Earth astray, while making war on the saints. John sees a beast rising out of the Earth, which supports the first beast.

[14]The lamb stands with His people, and they sing a new song before God's throne. Three angels fly over the Earth and they tell people the gospel, and about the defeat of Satan, and the reality of hell and judgement. This is a call for the endurance of the saints. Jesus swings a sickle across the Earth to reap the harvest of the Earth. [15]God's people stand by a sea of glass and sing praises to God. Seven angels with seven bowls/plagues come to finish off God's wrath. [16]The seven angels pour

out their bowls, and God's wrath is poured upon the Earth, bringing great destruction and anguish upon the Earth. [17]John sees a great prostitute and a beast, who are opposed to God, and will be conquered by the lamb, Jesus. [18]Angels from heaven pronounce the destruction of Babylon (sin) and all that trust in it. [19]God's people praise Him for his righteous judgements. The marriage supper of the Lamb and the Bride is fast approaching. Jesus, riding on a white horse, with all the armies of heaven, conquers those opposed to Him.

[20]An angel seizes the dragon and binds him for a thousand years. Jesus and His people reign for a thousand years, then the dragon is released and deceives the nations and makes war with Jesus, but the dragon is thrown into the lake of fire, along with all whose names are not in the book of life. [21]John sees the new heaven and new Earth, where God reigns and comforts His people, who will be sinless and perfect and full of joy. [22]John sees the river of life and the tree of life in the new heaven. The vision ends.

Jesus tells John that He is coming soon, and that His people must follow Him and keep His word, and trust in Him, for anyone who does this is truly blessed. Surely Jesus is coming soon. Amen.

6115280R00095

Printed in Great Britain
by Amazon.co.uk, Ltd.,
Marston Gate.